JEWISH LIFE
IN ART AND TRADITION

JEWISH LIFE
IN ART AND TRADITION

Based on the collection of the Sir Isaac and
Lady Edith Wolfson Museum, Hechal Shlomo, Jerusalem.

Yehuda L. Bialer
Curator

Estelle Fink
Assistant Curator

Photographs by David Harris

G. P. Putnam's Sons. New York

To Sir Isaac Wolfson, whose deep religious feeling and manifold interest in scientific, artistic and educational endeavour, and whose particular attachment to and generosity towards the Museum of Religious Arts and Crafts at Hechal Shlomo, have made the museum's collection and this book possible.

First American Edition 1976
Copyright © 1975 by Hechal Shlomo

Design by Alex Berlyne
Library of Congress Catalog Card number: 75–33424
SBN: 399–11695–8
Filmset by Keyspools Limited, Golborne, Lancashire, England
Printed in Great Britain by Westerham Press Limited, Kent

Contents

PUBLICATION OF THIS ALBUM will fill a long-felt need for the synagogue, the community and the individual. Based as it is on the Sir Isaac and Lady Edith Wolfson Museum at Hechal Shlomo, it is not just a catalogue of exhibits taken at random from the museum; it has a very specific pattern – or even a number of interwoven patterns. Essentially, the album constitutes the life-cycle of the Jewish man and woman from birth to death. Even as every age of Jewish history is depicted in art and sculpture, so the influence of every age and every society is portrayed here.

We are indebted to Sir Isaac Wolfson, through whose generosity and keen interest both the museum and this album have come into being; to Mr Y. L. Bialer, the creator of the museum and its indefatigable curator since its inception, who both inspired and wrote this book; to Dr Zerach Warhaftig, M.K., who during his term as Minister for Religious Affairs and in the museum's infancy provided the first exhibits; to Mr Bialer's loyal and devoted assistant, Mrs Estelle Fink, not only for her talents and hard work, but for her willingness to regard every concern of the album as her own. We owe a debt to the book's photographer, Mr David Harris, for his fastidious taste and expert craftsmanship, and to the publishers, Weidenfeld and Nicolson, and especially their designer, Mr Alex Berlyne, for his acute aesthetic judgement, ardent work, patience and forbearance in seeing the album through to completion. Finally, permit me to express our appreciation to my own deputy, Mr Haim Klein, and to the hard-working technical assistant to the museum, Mrs Miriam Blittner; to all those others who gave their services and, together with the museum's staff, worked as a devoted and loyal team, may I express my deep appreciation. I am sure that the publication of this unique and exquisite album will give them that satisfaction which it surely gives me.

Maurice A. Jaffe
Executive Vice President, Hechal Shlomo

Introduction

One could view this book as a volume on Jewish art or as an album of
Jewish religious objects. Both assessments would be true but both would
be oversimplifications. For the illustrations in the following pages reflect
the hopes, yearnings and aspirations of the Jewish people throughout its
long and chequered history and portray the religion, culture, tradition
and philosophy of Jewish life. The course of Jewish artistic tradition, like
the history of the Jewish nation itself, began, ironically, in exile. The
biblical view of the foundation of the Jewish people begins with the
account in Genesis 12, where Abraham is transformed from the heir of a
Mesopotamian tribal chieftain into the patriarch of an entire new nation –
yet to be forged – through a covenant with God: '. . . I will make of thee a
great nation, and I will bless thee, and make thy name great. . . . Unto thy
seed will I give this land. . . .' (Genesis 12:2,7). Yet even before Abraham
had produced a single offspring, the promise was qualified, and he was
told in a dramatic vision: 'Know of a surety that thy seed shall be a
stranger in a land that is not theirs, and shall serve them; and they shall
afflict them four hundred years' (Genesis 15:13). Thus it was that even
before the Jewish nation had crystallized, it was confronted with this
prospect of exile. But the lesson of the paradox was clear: Israel was to be a
nation whose character and survival were to be contingent not on any
given territory or regime, but rather on the constancy with which the
people – wherever they were to be found – would abide by the religious,
social and moral precepts to which they were bound and would remain
faithful to their ancestral tradition.

The exile foreshadowed in Abraham's vision was the bondage of the
Jews in Egypt. There the conglomeration of tribes began to form into a
nation, and there the people of Israel developed an affinity for artistic
craftsmanship. The more talented among them acquired extensive
knowledge in a variety of fields, and they learned the theory of
architecture and participated in building the 'treasure cities' (Exodus
1:12). They learned the technique of casting, of wood carving and of
working with copper, silver and gold. They became skilful in the arts of
weaving and embroidery and in the fashioning of artefacts. They learned
to cut and set precious stones and how to prepare and use striking colours.

9

These skills were acquired in the service of the Egyptian Pharaoh, but after the Jews left Egypt and had received the Torah on Mount Sinai, when they set about building the Tabernacle in the desert, they were able to call upon talented professionals in their midst, men referred to in the Bible as the 'wise at heart'. Out of bits and pieces, these artisans succeeded in designing and constructing a building that would withstand the shifting sands of the desert, and they furnished it with beautiful and artistic accessories. The Bible dwells in great detail on the creation of magnificent utensils for the Tabernacle and the clothes worn by the High Priest (Exodus 25–8). There in the desert, one can find the source of the Jewish artistic tradition that has prevailed for centuries and is still followed today: the fashioning of ritual utensils and holy vessels, whether for the synagogue or the home.

Israel's history is like a broad river that has flowed for thousands of years through all the countries of the East and West, imbibing ideas, customs and artistic currents along its way and merging them with the original values of the nation. But despite the variety of foreign influences, Jewish artists have always been committed to preserve the indigenous Judaic spirit in their work. The predilection for original artistic creativity – born in exile – thrived when the Jews again found themselves in exile, now dispersed over the known world. After the destruction of Jerusalem and the Second Temple in 70 CE, and particularly after the failure of Bar-Kokhba's revolt against the Romans in 135 CE, Jewish art turned to historical and biblical themes, employing allegorical symbolism with messianic overtones. This was also the time when the synagogue began to come into its own as one of the fundamental institutions of Jewish communal life, and much artistic energy was focused on it. These themes, for example, first appeared in wall paintings in synagogues (such as the Dura Europos synagogue in Syria), in mosaics and reliefs and later on holy vessels and other objects. The talmudic sages, who flourished in the first centuries after the destruction of the Second Temple, stressed the aesthetic aspect of fulfilling ritual commandments, a viewpoint derived from the verse: 'He is my God and I will glorify him. (Exodus 15:2), which they interpreted as a prescription to enhance the performance of God's commandments by performing each act in an aesthetically pleasing manner. In the light of this maxim, Jewish artisans broadened the scope of their interest in 'ritual utensils' to include candelabra, Hanukkah lamps, spice boxes, wine goblets and the like and to fashion them in silver and gold. The same motivation encouraged people to commission beautiful utensils and objects not only for the synagogue, but also for personal use in the home on the Sabbath and holidays.

The work of Jewish artisans was also influenced and informed by the traditional books they had studied in the normal course of their education, and they devised modifications and variations on the symbols and sayings appropriate to the purpose of each object and the occasion for its use. The spiritual ties to the Land of Israel likewise inspired them to embellish their work with illustrations of holy places, such as the Western Wall, the Temple Mount, the Tomb of Rachel and so forth. The seven-branched candelabrum appears most frequently on Hanukkah lamps, wine goblets, *mezuzot*, trays, rings and other objects. Jewish craftsmen were also influenced by their immediate environment, and beautiful public buildings served as models for their work. Thus spice boxes were fashioned in the form of towers, and Hanukkah lamps in both the East and the West were modelled on architectural forms prominent in the local surroundings. These objects were kept in conspicuous places and lent a unique charm to the Jewish home throughout the year.

The photographs presented in this book are a testament to the vitality of an artistic tradition that has informed Jewish life since the construction of the Tabernacle in the desert. Most important of all, however, they illustrate how closely the creative impulse is and always has been bound up with the faith and perfect fidelity to ritual that have preserved Judaism as an entire way of life and the Jews as a people.

NOTE ON DATES
Throughout the text of this book the Jewish terms BCE
(Before the Common Era) and CE (the Common Era)
are used instead of BC and AD.
They are directly interchangeable.

JEWISH LIFE
IN ART AND TRADITION

יהי אריך ונוק ודעת הכולל חו"ן וככולע בין חו"ד שהם עתיק ומוקב/

וכן יש"ס ותבונה הם ת"ת מכריע בשני בחינותיו זבין ח"וד שהם מקד

וגבורה וכן יעקב זרחל הם זו"ד המכריע בין נו"ה בשתי בחינותין

שהם חו"ן כנודע איהו בגלם ואיהי בכוד. וכן זה מתחו

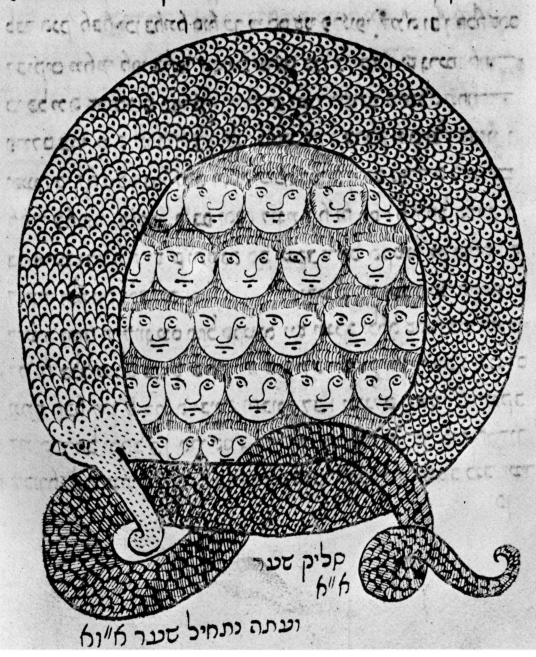

קליק שער
ח"א

ועתה נתחיל שער ח"ות

14

Founding a Family

OPPOSITE Allegoric illustration from *The Tree of Life* by R. Hayim Vital, illustrated manuscript, Central Europe, 18th century

Letters in the form of a fish, a common fertility symbol, from the above manuscript

China cup inscribed with the words '*mazal tov*' in gold and red, Germany, 20th century

For thousands of years the people of Israel have been supported by the pillars of two precepts in the Torah. The first is pronounced at the beginning of the Book of Genesis: 'Be fruitful and multiply', to ensure the biological survival of the nation. The second, pronounced at the end of the Book of Deuteronomy, is to study the law: 'Now therefore write ye this song for you, and teach it [the law] to the children of Israel: put it in their mouths. . . .' (31:19). These two basic precepts centre around the founding of a family, and that in itself is predicated upon the establishment of a marriage.

Marital partnership makes its first appearance very early in the Bible, in Genesis 2:18, where we read: 'It is not good that the man should be alone: I will make an helpmate for him.' Later, King Solomon stressed that it is the will of God that a man find a compatible woman: 'Whoso findeth a wife findeth a good thing, and obtaineth favour of the Lord' (Proverbs 18:22), and the talmudic sages also viewed matrimony as a felicitous state and maintained that a man without a wife 'abides without good, help, joy, blessing or atonement' (Yebamot 62:2).

The cycle of Jewish life therefore begins with the wedding ceremony, which is conducted in accordance with a pattern evolved more than 2,000 years ago, though with the passage of time, new customs that reflect changing social and economic conditions and contacts with many cultures have been incorporated into it. The bridal canopy (*huppah*) under which the couple is joined in matrimony is the most important element in the ceremony. Among Ashkenazi (European) communities, the canopy is an embroidered cloth stretched over four poles, resembling an open tent, whereas the Sephardi (Oriental) communities hold a prayer shawl taut above the heads of the bride and groom during the ceremony. The Ashkenazi wedding ceremony is traditionally held in the open, under the stars, for good luck, but when the ceremony is held in the synagogue, the canopy is placed above the platform (*bimah*) opposite the *aron ha-kodesh*, following the tradition of German Jewry during the Middle Ages. The Sephardi Jews traditionally hold the ceremony at home and lavishly decorate the house for the occasion.

For generations it has been customary for the bride to wear a white gown to her wedding. The groom, too, is clothed in a white robe (*kitel*) by the men who will lead him to the canopy. Like every custom deeply rooted in Jewry, this one has an ancient historic source. During the period of the Judges, it was customary for Israelite women to go out to dance in the city of Shiloh and for men to come and choose their wives from among the dancers (Judges 21:21). With the destruction of the First Temple in 586 BCE, these betrothal dances were abolished, but they were reinstated during the Second Temple period, when there was relative tranquillity in the country. These folk festivities took place twice a year, on the fifteenth of the month of Av and at the close of the Day of Atonement. For social and egalitarian reasons, it became customary for the girls who took part in the dancing, rich and poor alike, to dress in

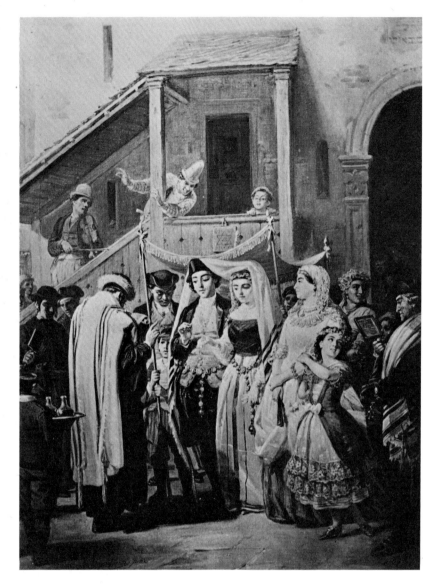

OPPOSITE (above) *Hitul* of painted cloth bearing the name of a child, Moshe Ben Aaron Friedrichstadt, Copenhagen, 1801; (below) triple nuptial belt, one for the bride, one for the groom and one with buckle to link them, gilded bronze with semi-precious stones, Germany, 17th century

The bride and groom wearing a nuptial belt, a painting entitled 'The Wedding' by M. Oppenheim, Germany, 1861 (Israel Museum)

LEFT Silver medallion cast in honour of the wedding of Helen Emanuel Milken and Joshua Leventhal of Frankfurt on Main, 1900

RIGHT Gilded copper medallion cast in honour of the wedding of Clara Weiskof to Moshe Shnarf, Frankfurt on Main, 1896

ABOVE *Swalef*, embroidered in gold thread on velvet, long black silk ribbons tied at nape of neck, Morocco, 19th century

ABOVE RIGHT Woman with festive adornment on her forehead and chest (*Brustuch*), painting by I. Kaufmann (1853–1921)

OPPOSITE (left, from top) Bride's headdresses: white silk embroidered in pearls, silver pins, diamonds, semi-precious stones, Poland, 18th century; pearls strung on white thread, diamond pin, Poland, 18th century; tiara with red stones, Russia, 19th century; (right) detail of woman's festive apparel, chest adornment, embroidered in gold and silver threads on brocade, Poland, 18th century

white garments. Daughters of needy families were thus saved from embarrassment. In antiquity a white garment was also considered festive attire to be worn during the holidays and particularly on the first day of the New Year and the Day of Atonement; in Orthodox communities men still don the *kitel* for the High Holidays and on Passover eve.

Before the nuptials there is a brief symbolic ceremony during which the bride's head is covered. Hair is considered to be a woman's natural adornment, and covering it symbolizes the change that takes place in her life when she relinquishes her single state for matrimony. From that point on, a woman's beauty is to be reserved for her husband alone, and covering the hair implies modesty and intimacy to the couple and indicates to the world at large that the woman is married. The groom and his best men, accompanied by the rabbi and members of the family, approach the bride – who is seated on an ornamented chair – and cover her hair and face with a veil. This custom has a biblical origin, for when Rebecca first met Isaac (who was destined to be her husband) 'she took a veil and covered herself' (Genesis 24:65). On the strength of this verse describing an ancient act, the Jews of antiquity covered the bride's head with a bridal veil (*hinumah*), and a virgin bride was veiled before she left her parents' home for the wedding ceremony.

Jewish women have always tried to invest imagination and taste in their

veils. In the talmudic period the veil was fixed to the head with a skull cap or diadem made of wool, silk or some colourful material embellished with gold or silver thread (Suta 49:2). The ordinances governing community life mention both those types of head coverings permitted to the Jewish woman and those forbidden, on social grounds, as being excessively ostentatious. In Italy, for example, wealthy women wore a net woven of gold threads and decorated their veils with expensive, brightly coloured feathers and artificial or live flowers. In Poland, from the eighteenth century on, a veil just covering the forehead, made of pearls, diamonds and other precious stones, was very popular. In North Africa the head covering, called a *swalef*, was fashioned of silver threads interwoven with horse or cattle hair or adorned with gold embroidery and coloured ribbons. The women of Bokhara used a triangular scarf that descended from the head to cover the back and was adorned with gilt spangles sewn to form the words: 'The voice of mirth and the voice of gladness, the voice of the bridegroom and the voice of the bride.' It was also decorated with replicas of fertility symbols, such as the fish, rooster or five-fingered hand. The wives of Orthodox rabbis used a head covering shaped like a black skull cap made of a closely woven net that would fit tightly on their heads after their hair had been shaved off. On holidays and festivals, the skull cap was decorated with a colourful silk tie and artificial

The bride being led to the
bridal canopy, copper etching
from a book by
J.C.Bodenschatz, Germany,
1748

flowers. Some observant women in our own day cover their hair only on
special occasions, such as when they light the Sabbath or holiday candles
or when they go to the synagogue or visit a holy place, while others wear
wigs at all times.

When the Second Temple was destroyed in 70 CE, the sages of the time
instituted the tradition of commemorating the fall of Jerusalem in the
words of the Psalm: 'If I forget thee, O Jerusalem, let my right hand
forget her cunning. . . . If I prefer not Jerusalem above my chief joy'
(137:5,6), and it has become customary to quote these verses on wedding
invitations. Where ancient Jewish customs are conscientiously observed,
before the ceremony ashes are sprinkled on the groom's head and the
bride divests herself of all adornment when she goes under the bridal
canopy in memory of the burning of the Temple (Batra 60:1). Other
local and familial customs that have become rooted in Jewry for many
generations are observed before the wedding ceremony. Among them is
the undoing of the bride's headdress, after which her hair is braided into
small plaits and silver coins are attached to the ends for good luck. Among
the Yemenites, the groom kneels before his mother, kisses her knees and
receives a silver coin from her, with which he blesses his bride.

When all the prescribed ceremonial acts have been completed, the
assembled crowd rises to its feet and, to the accompaniment of music, the

ברוילפט ‏אונ‏' שבע ברכות

א נאכט פור דער בריילפט זאגט מן
מין עטליכי קהלות קיין חתנה ‏׃‏ (לו
מ‏שט‏ניט דער חתן גוט דער טאו דער וויל
אן תחנה׃ זאגט ‏׃‏' רט אורגנט גיט אן ‏ל‏
אז אמין ‏׃‏ ‏חי‏ז דרומ דר מנהג רט דער חתן
זאל דער כלה זו גאר פריעאר זיין וואן ‏טר‏
מקרש ‏ו‏יי מוג דער חתן ‏כ‏אות זיא בייה
‏וות‏נט מו‏' ‏פ‏ידרט זים מין וויניג ‏׃‏ מו
‏פט רענ‏רט קהל ‏ז‏מרן מויל חתן מו‏
‏ג מו‏' זמנ‏ט פרו ורבו‏׃‏ רט שלום זמ‏ זיין
‏ו‏חין ‏י‏ דער פסוק ‏כ‏' השם גבולך שלום
‏ב‏ חטים ישביער‏׃‏ מין עטליכ‏' קהלות טוט
‏ך נעוט מי‏ רט זעובינ‏ קארן‏' רב‏ר נאך
‏ט ‏ב‏ריה עניים ‏׃‏ מו‏' חתן חגו‏ כלה זעגן
‏זיין וויניג כ‏'מ מגנדר‏׃‏ דער נאך נעמט
‏רב רען החתן מו‏' פ‏ירט חין וודר הין וו‏ח‏ק
‏רים פ‏ריפן נעמן רים מאן רים כלה זג‏' רים כלה
‏ודרט פ‏ינגרו פ‏ארי‏׃‏ רט קאוט הער פ‏ון

‏ה רם מי יצחק ‏ב‏יגענינט נחס זים רען זים ‏ט‏ליימר מו‏' רעאקט זיך רט פנים ‏לוז‏ן צ‏ניעית וו‏ענן ‏׃‏ מין

two best men (who must be close blood relatives and are usually the father of the bride and that of the groom) lead the groom to the bridal canopy and guide him to face in the direction of Jerusalem. If the wedding is held in Jerusalem itself, the groom faces the Temple Mount. Then the best men take lit candles in their hands and walk out to meet the bride, who is led by the two mothers. It is customary for the best men and the bride to encircle the groom seven times (in some places only three times), and then the bride is placed at the groom's right side.

The wedding must be conducted in the presence of no fewer than ten adults, to ensure that the occasion will be publicly known. The rabbi makes the traditional benediction over a glass of wine, adding the words 'Blessed art thou, O Lord, who hallowest thy people Israel by the rite of the nuptial canopy and the sacred covenant of wedlock' (Ketubot 7:2),

23

ABOVE Marriage contract on parchment, undecorated following local custom, Florence, 1744

OPPOSITE Marriage contract illustrated on paper, Persia, 1921

Marriage contract on parchment with gold, blue and violet illustrations framed in gold stripes, Usafi, Morocco, 1919

OPPOSITE Marriage contract drawn on parchment showing signs of the zodiac, Moses and the Ten Commandments and angels, Padua, 1712

ABOVE Marriage contract on paper decorated with paper cutouts (above is a tower surrounded by benedictions in micrographic script), Yezd, Persia, 1890

OPPOSITE Marriage contract on paper, illustrated with vegetation associated with Jerusalem (evergreens, palm trees, bushes and flowers) and the signs of the zodiac, Jerusalem, 1844

אורה
ויקר
ומעשה תהלה
והתן המעלה
אמן נצח סלה
מצא אשר
וימ...

וגדלה
וגדולה
ולנשיא התהלה
הכלה המעולה
ברינה ובגילה
מצא טוב
מד... י

בששי בשבת ששה ועשרים ימים לחדש אב בשנת חמשת אלפים ושש מאות תשעה ...
לבריאת עולם למנין שאנו מונין כאן במתא דהראת דיתבא על מבועי מיא ...
בריות ומעיינות מסתפקא איך התן וכחור אפרים בן שמעון אמר לכלתא בתולתא ...
דא דנן דהואי ... לאנתו כדת משה וישראל ואנא ... אפלח ואוקיר ואיזון ...
ואוזן ואפרנס ואכסי יתכי כהלכת גוברין יהודאין דפלחין וסוקרין ...
ומכסין ית נשיהון בקושטא ... ויהיבנא ליכי מוהר בתוליכי כסף זוזי מאתן דאינון ...
מזוני ... דחזו ליכי ומזונייכי וכסותיכי וספוקיכי ...
...
וצביאת ... מדת כלה דא ...
...
נדונייא דהנעלת ...
...
וכל קבל דנא אחריות שטר כתובתא דא ... נדונייא ...
...
וקנינא ... בכל שמיא דקנאה ...
...
וערבאי לכתובה דא כולה עיקר ונדונייא ...
...
ודלא כאסמכתא ודלא כטופסי דשטרי ...
...
כתקון חכמינו זכרונם לברכה
...

נאום ... נאום ...

OPPOSITE Marriage contract on paper, illustrated with floral designs, traditional verses and benedictions and signed by the scribe, Herat, Afghanistan, 1879

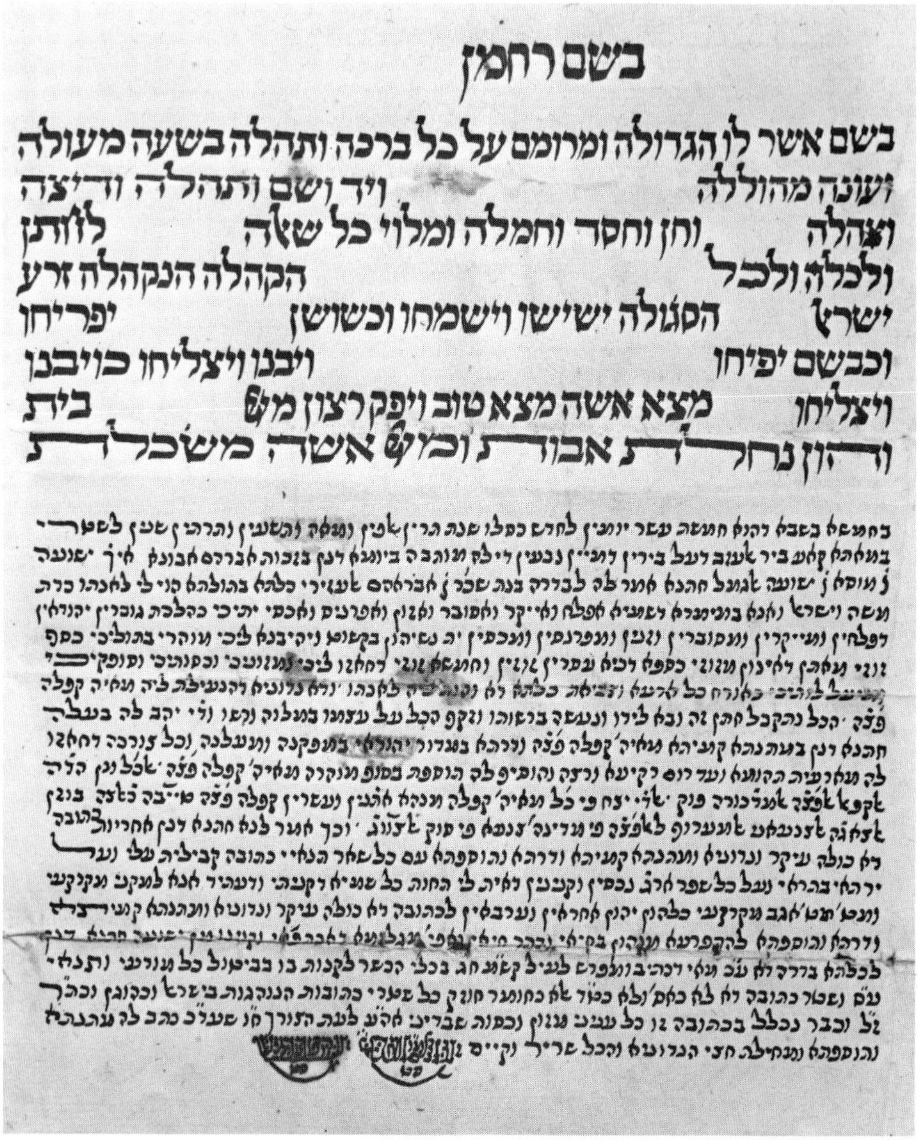
בשם רחמן

בשם אשר לו הגדולה ומרומם על כל ברכה ותהלה בשעה מעולה
ועונה מהוללה ויד ושם ותהלה ודיצה
וצהלה וחן וחסד וחמלה ומלוי כל שאלה לחתן
ולכלה ולכל הקהלה הנקהלה זרע
ישרא׳ הסגולה ישישו וישמחו וכששון יפריחו
וכבשם יפיחו ויבנו ויצליחו כויבנו
ויצליחו מצא אשה מצא טוב ויפק רצון מה׳ בית
והון נחלת אבות ומה׳ אשה משכלת

Marriage contract, hand-written on paper, Sana, Yemen, 1878

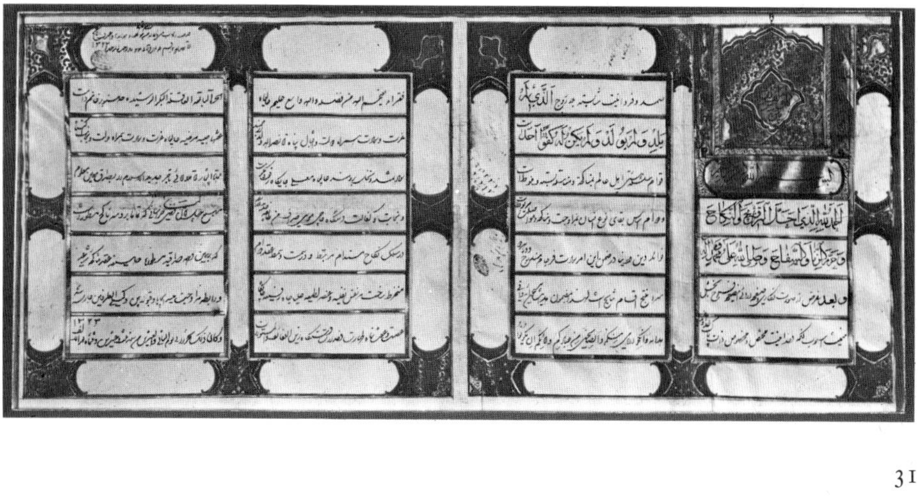

Marriage contract written in Persian on paper, Meshed, Persia, 20th century. This is a particularly important document as the Jews of this community were forced to convert to Islam but continued to observe Jewish customs and traditions in secret

ABOVE Marriage contract on heavy double paper, Damascus, 1849

OPPOSITE Samaritan marriage contract in three languages (Hebrew, Aramaic and Samaritan) in Samaritan square script, corner torn off as a charm ensuring peace in the household, Nablus, Palestine, 1913

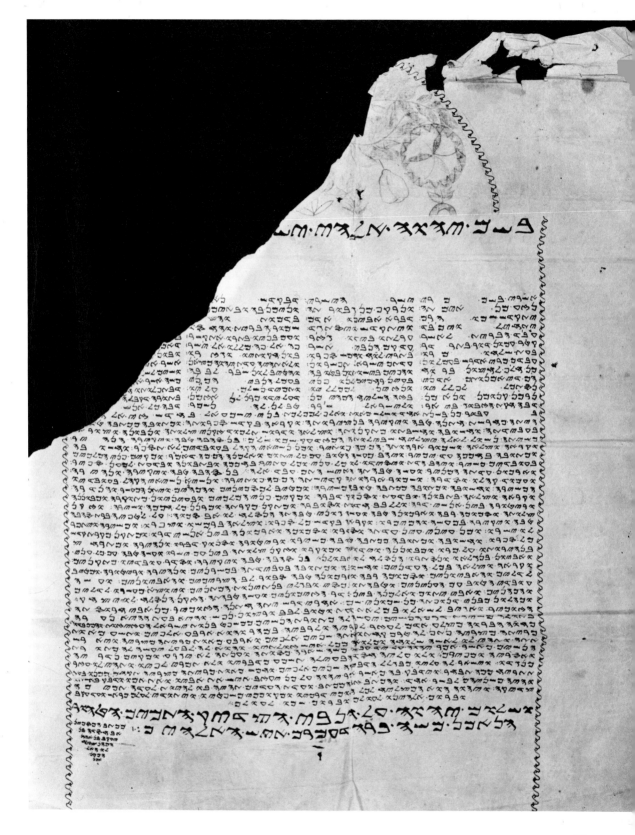

Woodcut from the book *Tzena Urena* showing Jacob rolling the stone from the well and Rachel approaching her father's flock, Amsterdam, 1766

OPPOSITE Title page of *Tzena Urena*, Amsterdam, 1766

and the bride and groom each sip wine from the glass. Then the groom slips a simple, unadorned ring on the finger of the bride's right hand and repeats the ancient phrase: 'Behold thou art consecrated unto me by this ring, according to the Law of Moses and of Israel.'

At the close of the ceremony, the groom breaks a glass. This custom originated soon after the destruction of the Second Temple, when the sages ordained that even on joyous occasions the nation's tragedy should not be forgotten. The manner in which the glass is broken differs from place to place. In Germany, for example, the groom throws it against the northern wall of the synagogue, shattering it against the stone on which are engraved the words: 'The voice of mirth and the voice of gladness, the voice of the bridegroom and the voice of the bride.' In the Portuguese community it is customary for the groom to break the glass in a bowl at the bride's feet. In most places, including Israel, the glass is broken underfoot. Influenced by the Kabbala and popular folk beliefs, various meanings have accrued to the glass-breaking tradition. Some consider it a charm to protect the couple against the evil eye on this joyous day, and, indeed, the traditional response of the assembled crowd is to shout '*mazal tov*' (good luck) in unison as the glass breaks.

צאינה וראינה בנות ציון

פירוש

חמשה חומשי תורה

מגילות והפטרות

אשר נלקט מכמה מדרשים שחבר המפורסם כמוהר"ר
יעקב בן כהר"ר יצחק ז"ל נדפס זה כמה פעמים
ברשיון והסכמת הגאונים אשר בימים ההם ולא נשנית אלא
בשביל דברים שנתחדשו בה · הלא המה ·

א דברי **אורחות חיים** לסדריך בית יעקב
בדרך טובים· **ב** **תפלה של שבת**
וכל הצריך לזה· **ג** שנדפס בכרך קטן למען יוכלו שאתו
כל איש בחיקו · **ד** שניתוספו בו **ציורים נאים**
להמשיך לב המעיינים· ומתוכם יבינו משמעות הענין
ועל כולם שנדפס באותיות חדשות ונייר לבן ודיו
שחור והגהה מדוייקת כאשר עיני המעיינים למופת יביטו:

באמשטרדם

בבית ובדפוס המשותפים

כהרר הירץ לוי רופא והתנו

קאשמן מוכרי ספרים

בשנת צאינה וראינה בנות ציון לפ"ק

After the ceremony the marriage contract (*ketubah*) is read. It sets out in detail the husband's responsibilities to his wife and the sum of money he guarantees as compensation in the event of divorce. This document was and continues to be written in Aramaic, the language spoken by the masses during and after the Second Temple period, underscoring the nation's desire to preserve its ancient heritage despite transformations in its way of life and the variety of tongues Jews have adopted during the thousands of years of their history. The contract is given to the bride for safekeeping, as it is forbidden for a man to live with his wife even a single day without it. The rabbi then pronounces seven blessings, known as the Seven Benedictions of Wedlock, which centre on three themes: thanks to the Lord who created man in His image and made of him 'a perpetual fabric'; a prayer to bring joy to Jerusalem by gathering her sons unto her; and commending the bride and groom to a life of joy built on four fundamentals: love, brotherhood, peace and friendship. After the ceremony the bride and groom leave the guests to be alone together, and according to traditional law, the most important aspect of the nuptial rites, the affirmation of the marriage, is this very privacy itself.

It is an ancient custom in Jewry, going back to the Bible itself, to present the bride with gifts before the wedding day. When Eliezer, Abraham's servant, came to Bethuel to ask the hand of his daughter for Abraham's son Isaac, 'the servant brought forth jewels of silver, and jewels of gold, and raiment, and gave them to Rebecca' (Genesis 24:53). In European communities during the Middle Ages, the groom's gifts were brought in a festive manner. On the day before the ceremony, or even earlier, the rabbi and important community functionaries brought

The book of *Hannah*, handwritten on parchment, Germany, 1700

OPPOSITE ABOVE Binding of the book of *Hannah*, cast, pierced and engraved silver, showing the sale of Joseph (right) and informing Jacob of Joseph's fate (left), Germany, 1700

OPPOSITE BELOW *The Voice of Supplication* (prayers to be said by a woman in confinement, during birth and while nursing, in Hebrew and Italian), Trieste, 1824

לְעֲבוֹדָתֶךָ הַטְּהוֹרָה וְיַחְדָּו כֻּלָּנוּ
נְקַדֵּשׁ אֶת שִׁמְךָ הַגָּדוֹל הַגִּבּוֹר
וְהַנּוֹרָא כְּלָמְדָם תּוֹרָתֶךָ לִשְׁמָהּ
וּבְהַדְרִיכֵם בִּנְתִיב מִצְוֹתֶיךָ עֲשֵׂה
לְמַעַן שְׁמֶךָ עֲשֵׂה לְמַעַן יְמִינֶךָ עֲשֵׂה
לְמַעַן תּוֹרָתֶךָ עֲשֵׂה לְמַעַן קְדוּשָׁתֶךָ
יִהְיוּ לְרָצוֹן אִמְרֵי פִי וְהֶגְיוֹן לִבִּי לְפָנֶיךָ
יְיָ צוּרִי וְגוֹאֲלִי:

לֵידָה

Le done che vano dd asistere la
partorente birano la presente
יְהִי רָצוֹן מִלְּפָנֶיךָ שֶׁתְּהִי יוֹלֶדֶת

40

אֲבוֹתֵיהֶ שֶׁ הַגָּדוֹל הַגִּבּוֹר וְהַנּוֹרָא
שֶׁלֹּא תָּבֹא שׁוּם תַּקָּלָה עַל יָדֵינוּ
וְיִזָּכְרוּ לְפָנֶיךָ זְכִיּוֹת הָעֲנִיָּה הַזֹּאת
אֲשֶׁר תָּחִיל תִּזְעַק בַּחֲבָלֶיהָ וְאִם יֵשׁ
בָּהּ שׁוּם עָוֹן מְחוֹל לָהּ וּמְרוֹק אֹתוֹ
בַּמֶּה שֶׁנִּצְטַעֲרָה בִּכְאֵב הַחֲבָלִים
וְתַעֲלֶה קוֹל צַעֲקָתָהּ לִפְנֵי כִּסֵּא כְּבוֹדֶךָ
יִסָּתְמוּ פִּי הַמְקַטְרְגִים עָלֶיהָ וְיִכָּנְסוּ
לְפָנֶיךָ כָּל הַמְלִיצִים בַּעֲדָהּ טוֹב כְּמִדָּתֶךָ
לְהֵיטִיב לְהָגֵן וְלִבְלְתִּי הָגֵן וְיֹאמְרוּ
רַחֲמֵיהָ עָלֶיהָ כִּי אַתָּה עוֹנֶה בְּעֵת צָרָה
מֶלֶךְ רַחֲמָן עַל כֻּלָּם פּוֹדֶה וּמַצִּיל שׁוֹמֵעַ
וְעוֹנֶה

aricordi alla partorente
La pui saggia e quela che

ABOVE Bride holding
prayerbook received as
wedding gift, photograph of
painting by M. Minkowsky,
Poland, 19th century

ABOVE RIGHT Binding for
bride's prayerbook, pierced,
engraved, partially gilded silver
on blue velvet, Nuremberg,
18th century

OPPOSITE (clockwise)
Prayerbook in ivory binding,
Moravia, 1891; prayer shawl
border, silver fret work,
Poland, 19th century;
prayerbook binding,
hammered and engraved silver
on velvet, Central Europe, 18th
century; woman's double tie,
velvet embroidered in gold
thread, Poland, 19th century;
prayerbook binding,
hammered and engraved silver,
family coat of arms at left,
Italy, 17th century

the gifts in the groom's name and, in accordance with the talmudic tradition, a 'feast of the gifts' was held on the occasion. In Yemen gifts were usually delivered to the bride's house in a gay procession to the accompaniment of drums and chants. Included among the gifts presented by wealthier families would be an artistic pendant made of gold-plated silver inlaid with precious stones, called a *labba* (heart). On the wedding day the bride hung it from her chin, and thereafter she wore it over her heart on festive occasions.

In Germany and Holland, in addition to rings and various jewels, the gifts included a double belt to be worn by the bride and groom under the bridal canopy. Sometimes the belt consisted of three pieces, one for the groom, one for the bride, and the third to bind the couple together after the ceremony. In addition to jewels and clothing, the Oriental communities also gave amulets as protection against the evil eye and evil spirits and to promote fertility. In Persia the bridal amulets were made of brass and were engraved with mystic combinations of letters and words, as well as the figures of a man and a woman. In Central and Eastern Europe, it was customary to give the bride a prayerbook in an elegant silver binding embossed with her initials or decorated with ivory and beads.

Books for women belong to a special category of gifts and are found in a variety of languages. There is the *Tzena Urena*, ('Go Forth and See'), a Yiddish translation of the Torah and other biblical passages for women who do not understand Hebrew. There is also the *Hannah*, which includes instructions guiding the woman in proper observance of the three specific commandments she is obliged to fulfil. Finally there is a book of special prayers pertaining to the various physical conditions in which a woman may find herself. These books are illustrated with woodcuts or etchings of biblical and historical scenes.

The groom's parents give the bride two silver, crystal or brass candlesticks to be used for lighting the Sabbath and holiday candles. There were communities where, on the first Sabbath of their married lives, the groom presented the bride with a gold ring, set with a ruby stone and engraved with a seven-branched candelabrum, bearing the inscription 'Kindle the Sabbath lights'.

LEFT Girl's hat (*gargush*), beaded with rosebuds and ribbons of gilded silver, pearls and velvet, Yemen, 19th century

OPPOSITE (from top) Box of hammered, pierced and engraved silver, North Africa, 19th century; bracelet, engraved gilded silver, Yemen, 19th century; necklace, enamel work, Morocco, 20th century; necklace, variety of beads, 19th–20th century; gold earrings, Iran, 19th century; gold earrings, filigree, Kurdistan, 19th century; ring of five silver rings joined by a jewelled clasp, Yemen, 19th century; ring, silver and coral, Yemen 19th century

OPPOSITE Necklace of ancient Egyptian gold coins, charms and golden beads, gems and corals strung on horsehair, Tunis, 19th century

Woman's headdress, silver threads interwoven with horsehair on cotton backing, coral beads, Atlas Mountains, Morocco, 18th century

Belt embroidered in gold thread on velvet, Morocco, 19th century

Bride's veil, tulle, triangular, with a portion of the verse 'The voice of joy, the voice of gladness . . .' and fertility symbols, embroidered in gilt and silver sequins, Bokhara, 19th century

בכור שורו הדר לו וקרני ראם קרניו

בסימנא טבא וכמזלא יאה אתחיל כג'לה ואנגמור כצהלה אורה והילולא ויקר וגדולה לחכמי הגולה לחתן הנעלה ולכלה הבתולה

בנין מצליחין ומעלה אמן נצח סלה ۰۰ מצא אשה מצא טוב ויפק רצון מה' הון ועשר נחלת אבות

ומה' אשה משכלת כי עמך מקור חיים כאירך נראה אור ۰۰ קרוב'ן אכ'ר

רביע בשבת בשלשה ימים לחורש אדר בשנת חמשת א---פים ושש מאורת ו----------משר---ה ועשר---

לבריאת עולם למנין שאנו מנין כאן במתא יזר דיתבא על סימ' באריתו ומעיינות מסתפקא איך החתן הנעים הבחור יחזקאל בן הכ' אשר הכהן

אמר לכלתא בתולתא בוגרתא כשרתא שרה בת הכ' שמואל הוי לי לאנתו כמו ۰۰ ואנא בס'עתא דשמ'א אפלח ואוקיר ואסובר ואיה

ואפרנס ואכלכל ואכס' ית'כי ליכי כהלכת כל גוברין יהוראין דפלה'יי ויוקרין ומסוברין זיגין ומפרנסין ומכלכלין ומפיסין ית נשיהון בקושטא ۰۰

ויהיבנא ליכי מהר בתוליכי כסף זוזי מאתן דאינון מזוז כספא רכיא עשרין וחמשא זוזין דחזו ליכי מנאי ומראויריתא ועל' מזוני'כי כסיתי'כי

וסיפוק'כי ומ'על' לוותי'כי כארח כל ארעא וצבי'את כלתא דא והוות ליה לאנתו כמו ۰۰ ודא נדוני'א דהנעלת כלתא דא מכית אביה בין בלבושין וב'

במאנין ותכשיטין הכל סך עשרין ארבּ' וצבי חתנא דנא והוסיף לה תוספת על עיקר כתובה סך עשרין ארבּ' והוי כל' מכון דכתובתא דא תוספּת

ונדוני'א בר מעיקר כתובה סך ארבעין ארבּ' הכל קבל עליו חתן זה וכא לירו ונעשה ברשיתו וחזק הכל על יצמו כמלוה ורשו ۰۰ וכך אמר לנא חתנא

דנא אחריות כתובתא דא וכולה עם שאר תנאי כתובה קבלית עלי ועל' ירתי בתרי להתפרע מן כל שפר ארג נכסין וקנינין דאית ל' מתחות כל

שמ'א דקנאי ודעתיד למקני ב'ה ממקר'קעי וממטלטל' ומטלטל' אגב מקרקע' כולהון יהון אחראין וערבאין לכתובתא דא לאתפריעא מנהון

כחי' וכתר חי' ۰۰ ואפילו מנלימא דאכתפאי באחריות כתובתא דא וקנינא מחתנא דנא במזל'ב ועל כל מא' דכתיב וספורש לעיל בקנ'יש מעכשיו

דלא כאפריכתא ודלא כטופסי דשטרי צ' כחומר וכחוזק כל שטרי הכתובות התהוגות בכנות ישראל העשויין כהוגן וכתיקון חזל וכתבנו וחתמנו

על שטר כתובה זו כזמן הנזכר למעלה והכל שרייר ובריר ונהי---- ונהיי וציק וישר וק'' וק'

שריריר וקיים
אשר אהרב
כתהר

עד עג'ף'צ'
מ'ל שער ראובן
לח'מ'ג'ב'

עד ---
---ר ראובן
כזא יצחק ---ון

עד ---
---חק ---

OPPOSITE Marriage contract on paper, Yezd, Persia, 1865

RIGHT Marriage contract, Diercasa, Leeds, England, 1943

בס"ד

אשר כגפן פוריה בירכתי ביתך בניך כשתילי זיתים סביב לשולחניך

מזל טוב בשעה טובה ומוצלחת

בחמשה עשר יום לחודש תמוז שנת חמשת אלפים ושבע מאות ושלשה לבריאת עולם למנין שאנו מונין כאן
ליידז איך מורינו ר' חיים צבי דמורינו ר' אליעזר אברן אחד לקדמנא ואמר לנא הדא מרת חיילא ר' חיים כד הוית בתולתא
זיבת לי לאנתו מן קדמת דנא כהלכות בנת ישראל דמוסבין לגוברייהן בחופה וקידושין ובכתובה וכדו איכפל לה סטר כתובתכ

והכל שריר וקים

נאום   עדים
ונאום

נפתלי בהרב ר' חיים שלמה
הנרע בשם חזן האלטער

ABOVE LEFT Mirror in prayer-shawl bag with a lion, symbol of the Persian Empire, on the cover, hammered, engraved and pierced silver, Persia, 19th century

ABOVE RIGHT Reverse of the same prayer-shawl bag, amulet of paper showing two candelabra with quotation from Psalms and the verse: 'Joseph is a fruitful bough'

RIGHT Back of mirror set in hammered and pierced silver with blue enamel, gift to bride as a charm for happiness, Persia, 19th century

Plate, amulet of engraved pewter with illustrations and quotations, Persia, 19th century

LEFT Wedding amulet, engraved brass depicting bride and groom, Persia, 18th century

RIGHT Wedding amulet, engraved brass depicting bride and groom holding a flower, Persia, 18th century

Passover plate presented as a wedding gift (*Einwarf*), engraved pewter with symbols of the *seder* (*matzot* and bitter herbs), quotations from Hagaddah and name of the artist decorate the border, Disburg, Germany, 1814

Passover plate, engraved
pewter bearing the inscription
'DD' (initials for *doron drasha*),
wedding gift to groom,
Prague, 1810

LEFT Container and brush for kohl, engraved silver, gift to bride bearing inscription: 'Behold, thou art fair, my love . . . thou hast doves' eyes' (Song of Songs 4:1), Persia, 19th century

OPPOSITE (from top) Marriage contract, six-page notebook illustrated in gold, violet, blue and pink, Teheran, 1909; 'three festivals' gold earrings set with precious stones, Bokhara, 19th century; fan, flag embroidered with sequins, Afghanistan, 19th century; wooden comb, drawing in style of Persian miniatures at sides, woman's face in centre and biblical verse inscriptions, Persia, 19th–20th century; gold earrings with enamel ornament, Persia, 18th century, medallion, agate, gold frame set with pearls and gems, pearl beads and three turquoise bangles, Meshed, Persia, 19th century

מצא אשה מצא ✦   בסימנא טבא בסיעתא
טוב ויפק רצון מה"   דישמיא ובמזלא יאה

Marriage contract, six-page
illustrated notebook,
Teheran, 1930

OPPOSITE (clockwise from top
left) Amulet, hammered,
engraved, repoussé silver, glass
and enamel beads, Morocco,
20th century; heartshaped
amulet, engraved, filigreed,
gold, pearls and precious
stones, pendant and two lockets
for amulets, Morocco, 19th
century; necklace, gold, three
strands, hands and amulets,
Tunis, 19th century; necklace,
almond-shaped droplets and
amulet of silver separated by
coral beads, Bokhara

Following customs that evolved among the well-to-do families of
Eastern Europe, the groom, too, is given appropriate gifts at specified
times. The bride's parents gave him a gold watch as a first token of the
engagement, and some time between the engagement and the wedding he
was given a Hanukkah lamp. If he was a scholar, he received twenty
volumes of the Talmud, the Mishna and the books of ethics. In Hassidic
circles, it is customary before the wedding to give the groom an elegant
hat made of expensive fur (streimel), which is to be worn at the wedding
ceremony and thereafter on the Sabbath and ceremonial occasions. On his
wedding day he receives a new prayer shawl with an embroidered border
of silver stripes and sometimes also a white robe (kitel) with a silver-
appliquéd collar to be worn at the wedding ceremony, on the High
Holidays and at the Passover seder. In religious circles in Eastern Europe,
where the young men were talmudic students, a special type of gift was
instituted. The groom was given a 'sermon gift' (doron drasha), an allusion
to the sermon he would deliver at both the wedding banquet and during
the seven festive days following it. In addition to useful and decorative
objects for the new house, it was also customary to give the groom a
Passover plate, a citron (etrog) box, a spice box and wine glasses for the
benedictions. These objects were lettered with the Hebrew initials of the
words doron drasha.

OPPOSITE (above) Necklace (*labba*), rows of filigreed pendants strung in strands, gilded silver set with sapphires; (below) necklace, silver filigree and coral beads joined to form triangles at tips, rectangle in centre, Yemen, 19th century

Sabbath ring, gold engraved with carnelian, bearing seven-branched candelabrum surrounded by inscription: 'Kindle the Sabbath lights', Central Europe, 18th century

Pair of candlesticks, hammered and engraved silver with the inscription: 'In honour of the Sabbath and holidays', Breslau, Poland, 19th century

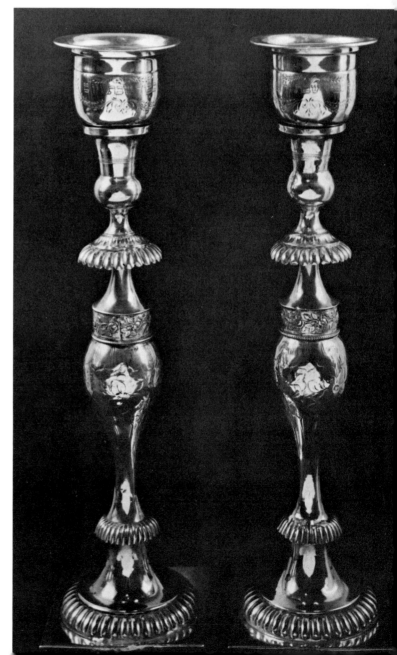

LEFT A Jew touching the *mezuzah*, affixed to the right doorpost, as he leaves his house, photograph from the Rothschild Miscellany, Italy, 1470 (Israel Museum)

ABOVE LEFT *Mezuzah* case, cast and hammered silver with parchment encased in a metal tube, Poland, 19th century

ABOVE RIGHT *Mezuzah* case, carved wood, depicting the Western Wall and Rachel's Tomb, Palestine, 19th century

The Home

The festive week following the wedding is soon over and routine life begins, with the couple facing the challenge of establishing a household. When it was still customary to give the son in marriage at the age of eighteen, as decreed by the rabbis in the talmudic era (Pirkei Avot 5:24), and the daughter at an even earlier age, to ease the initial period for the newlyweds the bride's parents undertook (in the betrothal agreement) to keep the couple in their home and provide for them for the first two years. During this transitional period the young husband, spared the burden of earning a living, could advance in his studies as well as prepare for his independence, while the young woman had the benefit of her mother's instruction and guidance in the running of a household. According to an ancient tradition, when a man reaches the age of twenty he must assume the responsibility for maintaining his own family and supplying all its needs.

Upon moving into a new house, the first command that a Jew is enjoined by the Torah to fulfil is to affix the *mezuzah* (doorpost scroll) at the entrance (Deuteronomy 6:9–11 and 20). The *mezuzah* on the doorpost is thus the distinguishing mark of every Jewish house. The text of the scroll is written in a stylized uniform script devoid of all ornamentation; it includes the main precepts of the Jewish faith and a warning against the pagan cults and beliefs that were so widespread in antiquity. The scroll is affixed to the right post of the doorway, slanting inward, indicating to visitors that they are welcome to enter.

Since the Holy Name is written on the *mezuzah* and the Hebrew word *Shadai* (a sacramental name for God) appears on its outer side, it must be respected and may not be exposed in an unclean place. In response to the unsanitary conditions of the streets and the presence of domesticated animals about the household, it became customary either to place the rolled parchment inside a hollow recess sunk into the doorpost or to cover it with a cloth. It later became a practice to enclose the *mezuzah* in a hollow reed or wooden tube and affix it to inner doorways. Seventeenth-century sources refer to glass tubes, and by the eighteenth century the well-to-do were already commissioning silver cases from artisans, while artistically designed cases of brass, ivory, stone and carved wood also became fashionable.

A different type of cover created for the same reason evolved concurrently in North Africa, where the *mezuzah* cover was made of coloured embroidery depicting a heart, shield, star, five-fingered hand or other symbols. In the centre of the cover is the word *Shadai* and the name of either the woman who embroidered the cloth or the one to whom it was presented as a wedding gift. At a later period covers of wrought silver lined with colourful velvet also appeared.

Just as the *mezuzah* is the distinguishing mark of the exterior of the Jewish house, so the *shiviti* plaque exemplifies the interior of the traditional household. As it was hung on the eastern wall of the house, in the direction of Jerusalem, it was also called a *mizrach* ('east'). Among the

Shiviti plaque, coloured paper cutouts, Galicia (Austria), 19th century

Oriental communities *shiviti* amulets are also widespread, as are pages called *menorah* because of the seven-branched candelabrum (*menorah*) pictured on them. The *shiviti* plaque has two functions. One is to remind man that there is an all-seeing eye and all-hearing ear and that his deeds are recorded in a book (Pirkei Avot 82:1), the other is to serve as a guide for individual prayer when one prays at home. *Shiviti* tablets were artistically executed on parchment, drawn on paper in the form of the seven-branched candelabrum, etched in copper, embroidered and printed.

The presence of decorative art inside the Jewish home in ancient times and the Middle Ages can be better deduced from the brief references

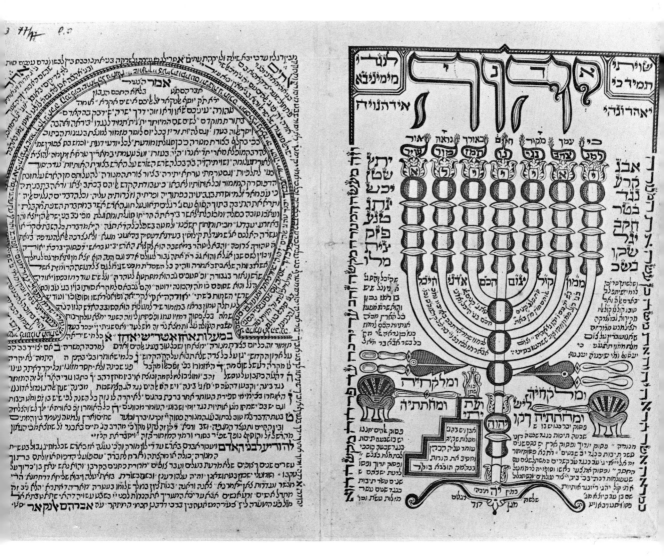

Shiviti plaque, copper etching on paper, showing the Temple candelabrum and its appurtenances with a Kabbalistic explanation, Algiers, 18th century

Amulet, silver filigree, displaying a building with two columns and a dome as a floral decoration, word *Shadai* in centre, Italy, 18th century

Amulet case, silver filigree, shaped like two-headed eagle with word *Shadai*, Italy, 18th century

dispersed throughout the Talmud and the books of later epochs than from the few extant examples that have been uncovered until now. From these sources we learn that the walls of houses inhabited by Jews in Palestine and Babylonia were decorated with pictures of the landscape around Jerusalem and of biblical scenes, as well as figures of animals and birds, accompanied by explanatory text (Shabbat 149:1). We also find references to coins (apparently medallions) with figures and symbols representing Abraham and Sarah, Joshua, Mordechai and Esther and so on. In addition, throughout the ages it has been customary to decorate the walls with portraits of famous rabbis and outstanding scholars.

The cycle of special events in the family begins with the birth of the first child. An atmosphere of mystery surrounded pregnancy, and folk fantasy invented fears centred on invisible evil forces that lie in wait for the mother and the new-born child. Naturally enough, the instinctive quest for protection created ways and means of warding off those hidden forces. Many and varied means were brought to bear, some basically religious in content and some psychological, depending upon the customs and traditions of any given community. Examples include bringing the *sefer Torah* to the home of the woman in confinement, the recitation of special prayers, pasting up pieces of paper inscribed with Psalm 121 or with nine verses of Psalm 20 (alluding to the nine months of pregnancy), vowing to contribute to the welfare of needy women in childbirth and writing the names of the demons Sanoi and Sansanoi and of the angel Samengelof.

ABOVE LEFT *Mezuzah* cover, embroidered in gold thread on red velvet and adorned with spangles, glass beads and the name of its owner, Morocco

ABOVE RIGHT *Mezuzah* cover, engraved, pierced silver, Morocco, 19th century

OPPOSITE (clockwise) *Mezuzah* covers: heart-shaped, embroidered with gold thread and spangles, Morocco, 20th century; shield embroidered in silver thread on velvet, Morocco, 19th century; *mezuzah* cases: carved ivory, Europe, 19th century; hammered silver, Austria, 19th century

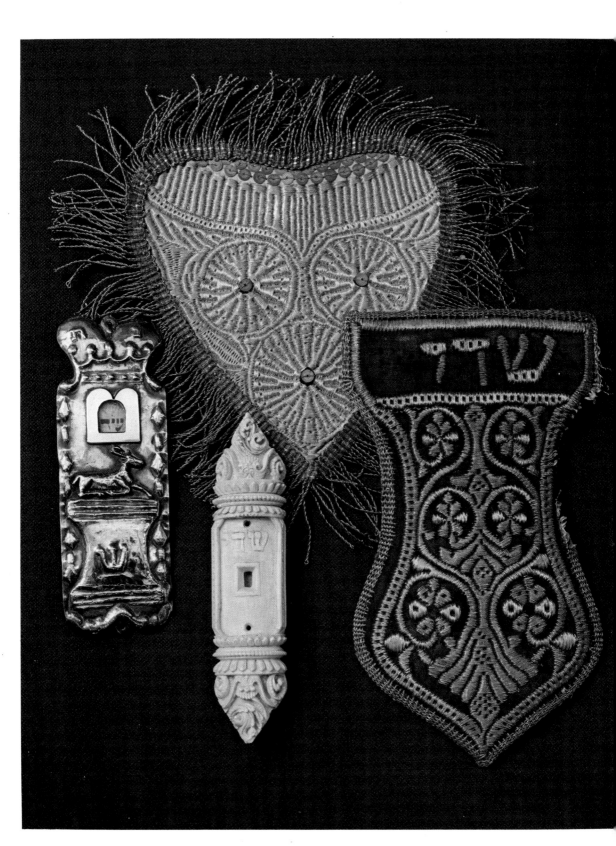

צורתהרב זה המוחר' יהונתן זצלאבר רס אלטונא המבורג ואנזיבעק

Portrait of R. Yehonatan Eybeschütz, rabbi of three communities, Altona, Hamburg and
Wandsbek, oil on canvas, Germany, 19th century

Portrait of a rabbi, oil on canvas, Bohemia, 19th century

Birth amulets
(clockwise): necklace for
pregnant woman, cast and
pierced silver, three pendants in
shape of a hand, two pendants
depicting infants of pearl and
enamel, Afghanistan, 19th
century; engraved silver with
turquoise stones, Persia, 19th
century; hammered and
engraved silver, coral beads,
Persia, 18th–19th century;
heart-shaped locket, engraved
silver, Morocco, 19th century;
buckle, engraved and welded
silver, precious stones, Persia,
18th–19th century; amulet in
form of a fish, hammered silver
with three pendants, one
shaped like a frog, Morocco,
19th century

Etching of four customs
associated with childbirth by
Kirshner

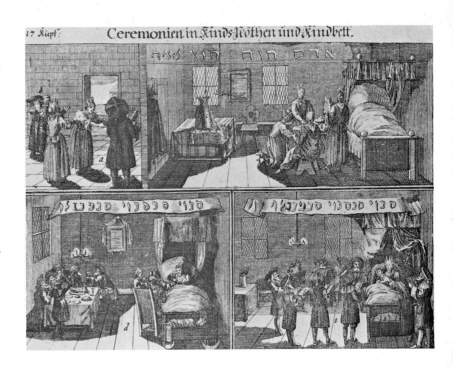

There was also widespread use of symbolic objects supposed to possess
remedial properties, the most popular of which was the amulet.

A set of traditional laws, ceremonies and celebrations that vary from
community to community and family to family were observed before
and after the birth. According to the medical conception prevalent during
the talmudic era, a woman is considered ill for thirty days after the birth,
and she therefore enjoys special treatment. Her ritual obligations are
lessened and she is relieved of all work. Custom ordained that she remain
in her house until the fourth Sabbath after the birth, which was called the
'arising' (*Aufstand*) by European Jews and 'the concluding Sabbath' by
Yemenite Jewry. On this Sabbath the new mother attended the
synagogue with her husband, who was called up to the Torah reading and
was greeted by the assembled worshippers with a cry of '*mazal tov*'.
In honour of the day, a reception with traditional foods was held for
visitors, and only after that did the woman resume her normal household duties.

Six-sided case for amulet,
silver, niello work inscribed
with names of angels and letter
combinations, Persia, 20th
century

TOP Amulet, engraved silver in form of convex cartouche, Persia, 18th–19th century

BOTTOM Amulet, engraved silver, fluted edge, two hooks, decorations and inscription, Persia, 19th–20th century

TOP Amulet, engraved and welded silver, inscription names of angels and owner, Persia, 18th–19th century

BOTTOM Amulet for mother and infant, engraved silver, image of demon Lilith in centre and surrounding inscription, Persia, 19th century

ABOVE Amulet for a woman, engraved silver in form of a stylized leaf, Persia, 18th–19th century

RIGHT Amulet against the evil eye, parchment hand-written in ink, Persia, 19th century

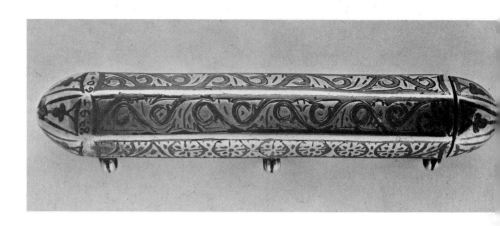

RIGHT Amulet case, silver,
niello work, six-sided with lid
and three hooks, Persia

BELOW Amulet, engraved
silver and blue enamel,
inscription in form of a
candelabrum, pendants shaped
like rosettes, birds' heads and
bells, Persia, 18th century

Amulet for a woman at childbirth, hand-written on paper with gilded wooden frame, protection against Lilith, Palestine, 19th century

Amulet for woman, engraved and welded silver and enamel with a chain and bells, Kurdistan, 19th century

The Circumcision Ceremony

In the Torah two acts represent the sign of the covenant between God and the people of Israel: observance of the Sabbath and circumcision. The circumcision is an individual, personal sign on the part of a man and his progeny. From Abraham onwards, for more than 3,500 years, Jews have performed the act of circumcision with a sense of intense spiritual uplift. As he enters into the Covenant of Abraham, the father of the nation, the child becomes part of the people of Israel, its faith, its destiny and its hopes, and the father therefore brings his son to be circumcised in fulfilment of a sacred duty.

The association of Elijah the Prophet with the circumcision ceremony derives from a collection of rabbinic literature, the *Wisdom of Rabbi Eliezer*, where it is written that until the kingdom was divided, circumcision was carefully observed in the Land of Israel, but when the kingdom of Jeroboam arose, the practice was abolished 'because the children of Israel have forsaken thy covenant' (I Kings 19:14). Elijah came and renewed that covenant, and God said to him: 'Thou hast faithfully observed circumcision; wherever my children perform this act, thou shalt be among them.' A chair of honour was thereafter instituted for Elijah, 'messenger of the covenant'.

A description of circumcision rites in the thirteenth century has been preserved in the *Mahzor Vitry* (625–6): candles are lit – 'for the commandment is a lamp and the law is light' (Proverbs 6:23) – and two chairs are prepared and covered with robes or a beautiful cloth. One chair is for Elijah the Prophet, who will be present at the performance of this good deed, and the second is for the godfather. The child is washed in warm water and dressed in fine clothes – a cloth shirt and overgarment

Memorial medallion, silver, gift of the *mohel* to infant he has circumcised, bearing a representation of Elijah's chair and the *mohel*'s name, Amsterdam, 1851

OPPOSITE LEFT The *mohel* Ya'akov Knaffelmacher's notebook, hand-written on paper, containing list of children he circumcised, Vienna, 1854

OPPOSITE RIGHT Perfume bottle, hammered, engraved silver, to sprinkle palms of visitors (custom of Oriental communities), Jerusalem, 19th century

and the same kind of ornate hat he will wear at his wedding. After a prayer he is ceremoniously carried to the synagogue and upon his entrance all rise and greet him with the saying 'Blessed be he who comes', and the person carrying him responds 'in the name of the Lord'. The child's father places him on the knees of the godfather, who is in his appointed chair, and the man ritually ordained to perform the act, the *mohel*, approaches and recites the benediction: 'Blessed art thou, O Lord our God, King of the Universe, who hast hallowed us by thy commandments and hast commanded us to make our sons enter into the Covenant of Abraham our father.' Then he cuts, uncovers the membrane and suctions off the blood. After that he pours a drop of wine on the penis and wipes it with a cloth dipped in olive oil, dusts powder on the wound and wraps the child in a large swaddling cloth adjusted so that he cannot inflame the area with his thighs. The *mohel* then washes and dries his hands. A glass of wine is poured and the *mohel* says the traditional benediction over it and adds: 'Our God and God of our fathers, preserve this child to his father and to his mother, and let his name be called in Israel [pronounces child's name] the son of [pronounces father's name], let the father rejoice in his offspring and the mother be glad with the fruit of her body.' The assembled respond: 'Even as he has entered into the covenant, so may he enter into the Torah, the nuptial canopy and into good deeds.' The *mohel* then drops some wine on the child's lips. Following the circumcision the child's legs are bound in a large swaddling cloth to safeguard the cut. More recently in Germany a circular piece of leather that could be tied with laces has been used.

Jewish tradition attaches great importance to the naming of the child. During biblical times the mother generally decided on the child's name, taking it from her personal background, but some women named their children after a contemporary historic event. In later epochs the most popular names were those of the Patriarchs – Abraham, Isaac and Jacob – the tribes, kings and other personalities of prominence in the Bible. Girls were named after the Matriarchs – Sarah, Rebecca, Rachel and Leah – and after Deborah, Naomi and so on. During the Middle Ages symbolic appellations, such as Arieh (literally lion), were adopted either in Hebrew or in the vernacular of the country in which the family lived. Ashkenazi Jews abstained from naming their children after a member of the family who was still alive, but in the Sephardi communities it was considered a great honour for the infant to be named after a living grandfather. As Jewish settlement was renewed in the Land of Israel in the latter half of the nineteenth century, the names that had been popular in the Diaspora gradually disappeared and biblical names of judges, kings and prophets came into fashion. With the establishment of the State of Israel, a new type of name with national overtones was introduced, and even the names of cities were adopted.

Paper cutout of benedictions and prayers for circumcision by Gabriel Bama and his son Leib, Weilun Synagogue, Poland, 1841

Embroidered decoration for circumcision ritual, gold thread on velvet, Germany, 1884

OPPOSITE Elijah's chair, carved wood, painted (partially gilded), with cushion embroidered in gold and inscription: 'Members of the Covenant of Abraham', Mantua, 18th century

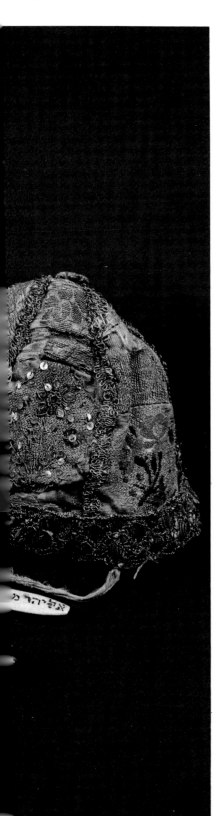

Special instruments and equipment were created for the circumcision, such as knives with silver, ivory or gold handles; some were even adorned with semi-precious stones and appropriate inscriptions or apt quotations from the Torah. There are also protective shields made of silver and brass and elaborately embossed. Of particular interest are the hand-written notebooks with artistically executed coloured illustrations in which the *mohel* recorded the names of the infants he had circumcised. From the large and varied body of material amassed on this subject in the course of the centuries, one sees how ardently and with what festive solemnity the Jews fulfilled the command to circumcise their sons.

LEFT (clockwise) Goblet for circumcision ritual, engraved silver with inscription: 'Glass of Elijah the Prophet of blessed memory', Syria, 19th century; *mohel*'s notebook of hand-written parchment with illustrations, Amsterdam, 1774; suction cup, gilded silver, hammered and engraved, Augsburg, Germany, 19th century; infant's skull cap, embroidered in silver and gold thread with sequins, Poland, 19th century; circumcision knife, handle of silver and ivory, inscription: 'Elijah, messenger of the Covenant', Turkey, 18th century: circumcision knife, handle of silver steel and bone, Germany, 1819; circumcision knife, engraved silver, Italy 18th century; circumcision shield, pierced engraved silver, Regensburg, Germany, 1843; circumcision shield, engraved silver, Persia, 19th century; powder container for circumcision in form of horn, silver, gold, niello work, inscription: 'Covenant of Abraham', Tola, Russia, 1845

ABOVE *Mohel*'s notebook, parchment, hand-written and illustrated, Italy, 1700

ABOVE Tray for redemption
ceremony, cast, engraved brass,
showing sacrifice of Isaac
surrounded by signs of the
zodiac, Poland, 19th century

RIGHT Redemption of first-
born ceremony, etching from a
book by J. C. Bodenschatz,
Germany, 1748

OPPOSITE ABOVE Page of
benedictions and prayers in
Hebrew and Ladino, Balkans,
20th century

Redemption of the First-born

The redemption of the first-born is performed in accordance with an ancient tradition that had its inception in Egypt. The Bible records that the first-born of Israel were saved from death by the epidemic that smote all the first-born of Egypt as punishment (Numbers 3:13), and when the Israelites left Egypt all the first-born were sanctified to the Lord (Exodus 13:2). Their special status was rescinded when the Israelites sinned in the wilderness by making the golden calf. The first-born were then replaced by members of the Levite tribe, who had taken no part in the sacrilegious rites (Numbers 3:12). When the Israelites began to effect the exchange by drawing lots – first-born against Levite – it became evident that there were 273 more first-born over the age of one month than there were Levites, and Moses was ordered to redeem the surplus at five *shekels* each (Numbers 3:47).

In our own times, the redemption of the first-born is effected by the same method that was ordained centuries ago. The father brings his child before a priest (descendant of the Levites) and announces that this is his first-born son. Following an ancient formula, the priest asks the father (in Aramaic) whether he chooses to give his son to the priest or to redeem him. The father declares that he wishes to redeem him, gives the priest a silver coin equal to five *shekels* and recites the specified benediction. The priest then accepts the coin and announces: 'Your son is redeemed.' It is

ABOVE Coin for redemption of first-born, silver, issued by Bank of Israel, 1970

RIGHT Redemption ceremony, copper engraving by B. Picart, Amsterdam, 1722

customary for the women of the family to bring their jewellery and adorn the child with it before the ceremony. Then candles are lit and a festive meal is held. At the end of the fourteenth century in the Rhineland, the Maharil instituted the custom of placing the sum for the redemption on a silver tray, whereby the father enhanced the good deed. This inspired artists of the eighteenth century to fashion a special silver or brass tray on which the infant is presented for the ceremony. In our own day, the Bank of Israel mints special coins (*shekels*) bearing an inscription appropriate for the redemption of the first-born.

The Bar Mitzvah

The day on which a boy reaches the age of thirteen is a joyous occasion for his family. According to the Talmud, childhood ends at this age and maturity begins. From the religious standpoint, the boy is henceforth viewed as an adult and '*bar mitzvah*' – accountable for performance of the obligatory precepts. He must observe the laws and perform the acts required of every Jewish man. The child prepares for this day for a year prior to the *bar mitzvah* ceremony. He is drilled in the sacred texts and the sources of Jewish lore and is taught the ritual of putting on the phylacteries. The significance of this rite, the content and sanctity of the phylacteries, their form and the way they are written are all explained to him. A bright boy is introduced to the major philosophic and ethical concepts of the act as propounded by scholars throughout the ages. He is taught that the phylacteries must be worn on a clean body and that it is forbidden to distract one's thoughts from them as they are being put on. On the Sabbath of the week in which his thirteenth birthday falls, the *bar mitzvah* is called up to the Torah in the synagogue, he reads the Portion of the Week from the Bible in the prescribed cantillation and concludes with

BELOW Pair of small phylacteries for head and arm with straps to wind around arm, 18th century

BELOW RIGHT One of the four portions of phylacteries below, parchment with inscription: 'Sanctify unto me all the first-born' (Exodus 13:1) in micrographic script, 18th century

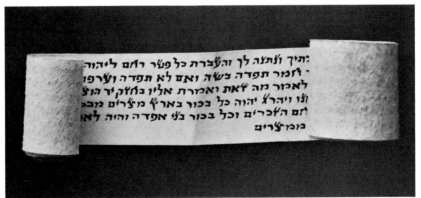

Page from the *Small Book of Positive Commands* by R. Isaac of Corbeil, hand-illustrated and written on parchment, containing the ordinances concerning phylacteries, France, 1313

a chapter from the prophets (*haftarah*) in traditional chant. In Orthodox synagogues, the girls of the family gather upstairs in the women's gallery and shower the *bar mitzvah* with nuts and sweets.

After the ceremony a festive meal is held, and if the boy is talented he is expected to deliver a discourse. He is presented with a pair of phylacteries, usually in a velvet bag on which his name has been embroidered; among the Oriental communities the first letters of the Hebrew words signifying 'servant of the Lord' are added. In North Africa it was also customary to give the boy a prayer shawl in an embroidered bag, sometimes covered with silver foil on which were wrought his name and biblical verses. In Poland wealthy parents also gave the *bar mitzvah* a prayerbook in an artistic silver binding and boxes in which the phylactery for the head and the arm could be kept separately.

In antiquity it was customary to wear the phylacteries on the head and the arm during the entire day, removing them only at night. Men even went into battle wearing them. The Talmud relates that after the revolt of Bar-Kokhba against the Romans in the second century, forty *seah* (a measure of the time) of phylactery boxes belonging to the casualties of the battle of Betar were found on the battlefield. The rabbinical sages realized that it was difficult to guard the phylacteries properly over a long period of time and to keep one's mind on them constantly, so they provided that with the exception of the Sabbath and holidays, they would be worn only at morning prayer.

Prayerbook binding, hammered and engraved silver, depicting Jacob's dream, the sacrifice of Isaac, Moses and Aaron, a candelabrum, two figures with a sheep, and decorations, and inscribed from father to son as a *bar mitzvah* gift, Austria, 18th century

Cup and saucer, china inscribed in gold under glaze, Bavaria, 19th century

OPPOSITE LEFT Bible in German with artistic leather binding, gift from mother to daughter, Gruenwald, Germany, bound by Royal Bookbinders, Berlin

OPPOSITE RIGHT Embroidered dedication in German on fly-leaf of same Bible, silk thread on silk, 1905

Dein "Ja" sei wahr-
haft und dein "Nein"
sei wahrhaft, rede
nicht anders mit
dem Munde als du
in deinem Herzen
denkst. Der Frommen
Ja ist Ja und ihr
Nein ist Nein.

Bag for prayer shawl, pierced and engraved silver on red velvet background, inscription: 'Servant of God, Nissim Bar Eliyahu Batbul', Morocco, 19th century

OPPOSITE Bag for phylacteries, *bar mitzvah* gift, green velvet embroidered in gold and silver thread, inscription: 'Servant of God, Ya'akov Beer', Morocco, 20th century

ABOVE The *bar mitzvah* delivering a sermon to his family and guests, engraving by M. Oppenheim, Germany, 19th century

LEFT Wine goblet for *bar mitzvah*, engraved silver, Lvov, Austria, 1857

OPPOSITE (clockwise) Bag for prayer shawl, pierced and repoussé silver, velvet, Morocco, 20th century; pair of phylactery containers, engraved silver, Poland, 20th century; phylacteries case, velvet embroidered in gold thread, Morocco, 20th century; pair of phylactery containers, filigreed silver, Poland, 20th century; bag for prayer shawl, velvet embroidered in gold thread, good luck symbols and decorative design, Morocco, 1936

Education

Educating the children in the Torah is compulsory in Jewish tradition and is the father's duty. As soon as the child begins to talk, his father is obliged to teach him the verse: 'Moses commanded us to learn the law, heritage of the congregation of Jacob', as well as 'Hear O Israel, the Lord is our God, the Lord is One.' Even in antiquity, every boy knew how to read and write. In Yemen, where there was a severe shortage of books, the one that was possessed by each class was placed in the centre of the room, and the children sat in a circle around it and learned to read from every angle, even upside-down. So important was a proper education that the sons of poor families received free education. When the child was three years old he began to learn the forms of the alphabet and the rudiments of reading.

The curriculum and the duration of each course were fixed in the Talmud. A five year old was to study the Bible and a ten year old the Mishna (Pirkei Avot 5). In the course of two years, the child was to have learned to read correctly and began the study of the Torah; at this point a celebration was held at the school called the 'feast of the Torah', and the child received gifts. In the Middle Ages the order was changed. The child was first taught the Torah with the commentary of R. Shlomo Hatzarfati (Rashi) and only selected portions of the prophets and Hagiographa, a system still followed. When the child was ten years old he was sent to another school to study the Mishna. When he became accustomed to the subject matter and language of the Mishna, he began to study the Talmud.

Girls also received a fitting education in the Jewish home and, when still very small, began to attend the synagogue. They learned the laws of ritual purity of foods (*kashrut*), specific rules and ordinances pertaining to women, and reading and writing. There were differences of opinion regarding the sacred books that girls should study, but eventually it was decided that they were permitted to study the Torah, but not the Talmud.

OPPOSITE *Hitul* for *sefer Torah*
in name of Ben Aaron
Friedrichstadt drawn on cloth,
Denmark, 1801

Ceremony of child presenting *hitul* for
the *sefer Torah*, engraving by
M.Oppenheim, 19th century

Letters of the alphabet and verses of the
Torah written on parchment as a
reading primer, Jerusalem, 19th century

Page for instructing small children,
letters of the alphabet and benedictions,
print and woodcut on paper, scene from
the *Heder*, Leghorn, 18th century

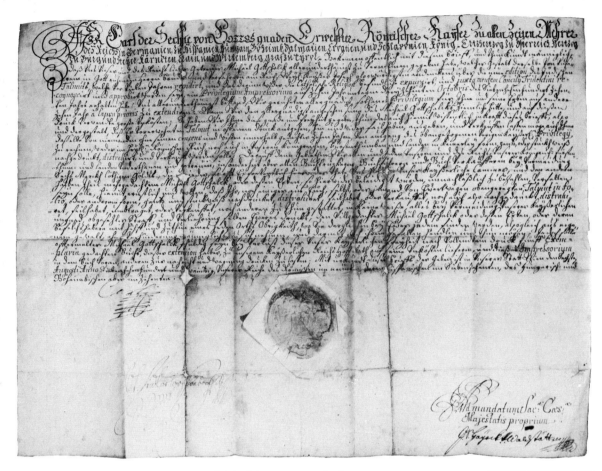

ABOVE Original documents conferring the privilege of printing the Talmud on the printer Michael Gotshalk with signature of the emperor of the Holy Roman Empire, Charles VI, paper on cloth, wax seal, Vienna, August 1720

RIGHT Title page of one volume of the Talmud printed in Berlin, Frankfurt on Oder, 1722 and authorized by the privilege

מסכת

מעילה וקנים ותמיד עם פירוש רש"י ותוספות ופסקי תוספות ומשניות עם פירוש הרמב"ם ז"ל

MASSECHET MEHILAH
Opus in qvo agitur de TRANSGRESSIONE
Recognitum à MARCO MARINO Brix. Can. Regul. D. Servatoris,
Et ab omnibus iis, qvæ contra Religionem Christianam sunt,
Juxta mentem Concilii Tridentini Expurgatum,
Adeò ut non modo citra Impietatem, verum etiam cum fructu legi possit:
Ante hac BASILEÆ editum,
Nunc secundum Editionem Basileensem
denuò emissum,
Cum Privilegio SACRi CÆSAR. MAJ. & Sereniffimorum
Regum POLONIÆ & PRUSSIÆ.

BEROLINI & FRANCOFURTI AD ODERAM
Impensis MICHAELIS GOTTSCHALCKII.

A child on his way to school to
begin the study of the Talmud,
sketch by Abel Pan

OPPOSITE LEFT Portrait of
R. Raphael Cohen, Chief
Rabbi of three communities,
Altona, Hamburg and
Wandsbek, aquatint etching,
Germany, 1798

OPPOSITE RIGHT Portrait of
R. Joseph Hahn, senior
rabbinical judge of the above
communities, aquatint etching,
Germany, 18th century

OPPOSITE BELOW Child being
tested by his grandparents on
the Sabbath, engraving by
M. Oppenheim, Germany, 19th
century

Portrait of R. David Nieto, rabbi of London, etching, England, 1705

The Synagogue

Wherever Jews are settled, the synagogue is the most important spiritual centre. Historically, the institution of the synagogue was founded during the Babylonian Diaspora after the destruction of the First Temple, and for 2,500 years it has served as a sanctuary and haven. It was the spiritual bond with the Temple in Jerusalem that inspired the establishment of the first synagogues in the Diaspora. After the destruction of the Second Temple, the people's longing for the Temple grew even more profound.

In his missive describing the beginnings of the synagogue, R. Sharira Gaon relates: 'After the destruction of the First Temple [in the sixth century BCE], the Jews were banished from Jerusalem with Jehoiachin, king of Judah, and reached the city of Nehardea in Babylonia. There they erected a synagogue and interred in its foundations stone and ashes brought with them from the ruins of the Temple.'

In Babylonia the synagogue served the exiles as a meeting place for prayer, and when they prayed they faced Jerusalem. The Jews who returned to Jerusalem with Ezra and Nehemiah after the proclamation of King Cyrus brought the concept of the synagogue with them and built synagogues after the Babylonian pattern in the cities of Judah and in Jerusalem. Even after the Second Temple was completed, local synagogues were a powerful force in strengthening and consolidating the religious and social life of the Jews in Judah. The customs and traditions that crystallized in that period have been preserved, and in broad outline the entire Jewish people adheres to them to this day.

The atmosphere characteristic of the synagogue is created primarily by its functional appurtenances and their adornment. Its furnishings, holy vessels, decorations, rugs and tapestries and symbols have been bequeathed by generations past and bear reference to the dramatic events experienced by these generations throughout the nation's history. From its beginnings the synagogue has been based on an ideology synthesizing two major aspects: in the presence of the entire congregation, each

Memorial medallion of synagogue dedication, cast silver, Munich, 1887

Alms box from synagogue in Piotrkov, Poland, 19th century

Interior of synagogue in Leghorn (destroyed during Second World War), combination of coloured marble and precious stone, etching, 1789

Pitcher and bowl for the priests to wash their hands in the synagogue, Germany, 19th century

individual concentrates on his own prayer, and the entire congregation listens intently to the reading of biblical texts and a translation and explication of them. Both aspects are still present today (only the translation that at one time accompanied the reading has been abolished. Instead, the talmudic sages instituted the provision that each worshipper must read the prescribed Portion of the Week himself, twice in the Hebrew original and once in the Aramaic translation rendered in the first century by Onkelus the Proselyte).

The manner in which worship in the synagogue is conducted restricted services to two focal points, and these determined the placement of the building's major physical elements: the platform (*bimah*) and the *aron ha-kodesh*. The function of the platform – occasionally referred to in Jewish literary and legal sources as the 'box' – is an acoustic one, according to Maimonides, 'So that all will hear equally'. Traditionally its place is in the centre of the synagogue. The Kabbala interprets the platform as a symbol of Mount Sinai, which the reader or the rabbi ascends. On the New Year

RIGHT *Aron ha-kodesh*, gilded wood, from the Kasis family's synagogue, Mantua, 18th century

BELOW Eternal light of a synagogue, filigreed silver, Italy

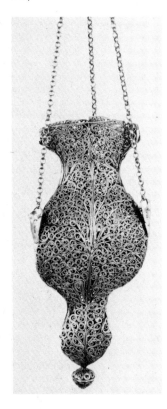

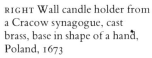

RIGHT Wall candle holder from a Cracow synagogue, cast brass, base in shape of a hand, Poland, 1673

OPPOSITE Doors of the *aron ha-kodesh* of Wolff Poper (Butzian) Synagogue, carved and painted wood with inscription from Pirkei Avot, Cracow, 17th century

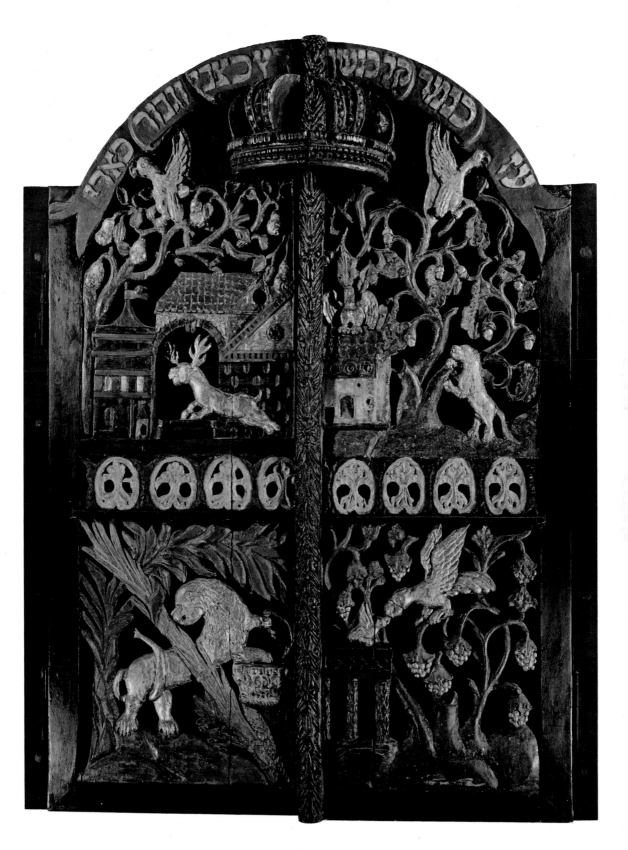

OPPOSITE *Shiviti* parchment,
frame of carved and fretted
wood, from synagogue in Old
City of Jerusalem, 19th century

Drawing of interior of
synagogue in Safed by
M. Levanon, *gouache*, 1962

Drawing of interior of synagogue in Halberstadt, Germany, watercolour, 19th century

OPPOSITE (clockwise) Torah crown, hammered, gilded silver with precious stones, amber hanging in centre, Poland, 18th century; Torah crown, hammered, engraved partially gilded silver with precious stones, Ukraine, 18th century; Torah crown, gold adorned with precious stones, Amsterdam, 19th century; *yad l'Torah*, partially gilded, filigreed silver, Poland, 19th century

LEFT Wall lamp in Sephardi synagogue, hammered and engraved tin and brass, Holland, 18th century

RIGHT Medallion showing bust of R. Eliezer of Brody, who was appointed Chief Rabbi of Amsterdam, cast copper, Amsterdam, 1735

Me'il, velvet, gold and silver thread and wool decorated with seven-branched candelabrum, utensils of the Tabernacle, Tablets of the Law, the Ten Commandments and the names of the donors, Germany, 1748; (above) Torah crown, hammered silver, Poland, 18th century; (left) *yad l'Torah* shaped like silver baton, Europe, 19th century

OPPOSITE *Parochet*, velvet embroidered in gold and silver thread, Germany, 1716; buried in the ground and thus saved during the Holocaust

זה השער לי' צדיקים באום

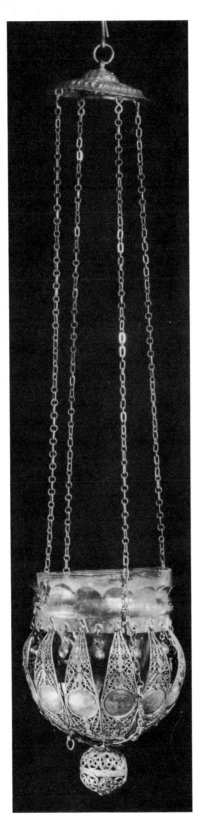

OPPOSITE Wall carpet from Sephardi synagogue, wool and silk thread, inscription: 'This is the gate of the Lord the righteous shall enter', Turkey, 17th century

LEFT Eternal light, hammered, engraved filigreed silver, emblem and names of the tribes on cartouches, Morocco, 20th century

RIGHT *Tik*, hammered and gilded silver, Basra, Iraq, 1904

OPPOSITE LEFT *Rimonim*, engraved silver, Yemen, 19th century

OPPOSITE RIGHT Pendants, engraved silver, hung around the *sifrei Torah* to indicate in which order they should be used in the service, Rangoon

OPPOSITE LEFT Flag head in form of hand, engraved silver, amulet borne at top of a standard and carried during pilgrimages to the tombs of prophets and saints, Mandalay, 1896

OPPOSITE RIGHT Dedication plaque for the *sefer Torah* of the Beth El Synagogue, Shanghai, cast silver, China, 1885

RIGHT *Tik*, hammered, partially gilded silver, coral and wood with stylized lotus leaves, Calcutta, 1852; (above) *rimonim,* gilded silver, Rangoon

Pair of synagogue oil lamps, cast bronze, Cochin, 1719

Book of *Tashlich* prayers for the New Year in the script used by Cochin Jews, 20th century

OPPOSITE Synagogue candelabrum, cast brass and glass shaped like Shield of David with cups for oil and six hands (*hamsot*) on chain, Morocco, 20th century

Sabbath and holiday lamp, cast and engraved brass, Cracow, 19th century

the *shofar* (ram's horn) is blown from this raised platform in commemoration of the Revelation at Sinai and the giving of the Torah, following the verse: 'And when the voice of the *shofar* sounded long, and waxed louder and louder, Moses spake, and God answered him by a voice' (Exodus 19:19). In some ancient synagogues sculptured lions flanked the platform as they had once flanked Solomon's throne: 'And there were stays on their side on the place of the seat, and two lions stood beside the stays' (1 Kings 10:19). The remains of stone lions have been found among the ruins of synagogues uncovered in excavations.

The *aron ha-kodesh* is placed opposite the platform on the wall facing Jerusalem. The *sefer Torah*, which is read before the congregation at set times, is kept in the *aron ha-kodesh*, in some places built into the wall and in other places constructed of wood as a separate piece of furniture. The place in which the Torah is kept is not holy in itself, as in Jewish thought material objects are not sanctified; they are hallowed by what they contain – in this case the sacred Scrolls of the Law.

Traditionally the objects used for religious observance are divided into two categories: 'holy vessels' and 'ritual utensils'. Appurtenances directly associated with the Torah belong to the first category and those used for fulfilling ritual acts in the synagogue and the home throughout the year belong to the second. The holy vessels are the *tik, mapah, me'il, yad l' Torah,* crown, fringe, diadem, breastplate and *rimonim*.

Artistic embroidery is used extensively in the interior decoration of the synagogue. Delicate, brilliantly coloured embroidery adds splendour to the edifice, and the themes depicted coincide with the symbols and order of the prayers recited at services. These woven cloths and embroidered curtains are part of a hallowed tradition that began in the earliest days of the people of Israel. The curtain that covered the Ark of the Covenant and the skilfully embroidered hangings in the Tabernacle of the First and Second Temples, the cloth and silk Torah bindings mentioned in the Talmud, commentaries and the works of Josephus, as well as in mediaeval Jewish literature, have excited the imaginations of Jewish artists, who have produced a rich treasury of beautiful objects – many of which are on display in museums and synagogues today. The *parochet* before the *aron ha-kodesh* is particularly outstanding, but the memorial rugs and those covering the reading table and the cantor's stand are no less interesting and impressive in their beauty. In the Sephardi synagogues the *tik* and *mapah* of the *sefer Torah* and the woven and embroidered wall rugs are of rare splendour in design and execution.

In addition to lamps for illumination and skilfully wrought silver or brass memorial candlesticks for the deceased, every synagogue has a seven-branched candelabrum (*menorah*) and an eight-branched candelabrum to be kindled with either tallow candles or oil during the eight days of Hanukkah. Reproduced here is an eighteenth-century brass candelabrum from Poland, one of two that were in the Great Synagogue in Warsaw until the outbreak of the Second World War. The Jews managed to remove and bury it before the Nazis bombed the beautiful synagogue. Mrs Marguerite Wenner-Gren purchased it and donated it to the museum.

OPPOSITE Hanukkah lamp from a synagogue, cast and engraved brass, Poland, 18th century

TOP *Caporet* from 'Zagoiner Shul' synagogue, velvet, gold and silver embroidery, Prague, 1814

LEFT *Me'il*, brocade, velvet, embroidered in gold, silver and silk thread, Wielun, 19th century

RIGHT Etching of old 'Altneushul' Synagogue, Prague

Painting of interior of 'Altneushul' Synagogue, Prague, oil on
canvas by C. Grueb, 1876

ABOVE Couple in Jewish attire, coloured etching, Frankfurt on Main, 18th century

ABOVE RIGHT Goblet, gold inlaid with precious stones and with inscriptions, work of Meister Horowitz, Frankfurt on Main, 1928

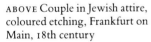

RIGHT Title page of book about the Talmud, *Blessings of Judah*, printed in Frankfurt on Main, 1704

ABOVE Breastplate for *sefer Torah*, cast and pierced silver, Frankfurt on Main, 18th century

LEFT Interior of synagogue in Frankfurt on Main, aquatint etching, Germany, 19th century

View of the 'Turkish
Synagogue', Vienna, coloured
aquatint by G. Wolf, 19th
century

LEFT Medallion in memory of
Rabbi A. Jellinek (1820–98),
bronze, Vienna

RIGHT Medallion in memory of
Rabbi J. N. Mannheimer, bronze,
Vienna, 1789

OPPOSITE *Rimonim*, cast and
hammered silver, Vienna, 1883

Rimonim, hammered, filigreed silver, Holland, 18th century

Diadem for *tik*, hammered and engraved silver, Rhodes, 19th–20th century

OPPOSITE Torah crown, partially gilded, hammered, engraved, cast and pierced silver with precious stones, Poland, 1695

ABOVE Torah breastplate, pierced and engraved silver, Turkey, 19th century

LEFT Synagogue candelabrum, cast brass, glass, inscription in gold, hook in form of hand, Morocco, 19th century

Torah crown, partially gilded, hammered, engraved, cast
and pierced silver, Morocco, 19th century

RIGHT *Rimonim,* carved wood, gilded, in Oriental architectural style, Morocco, 18th–19th century

ABOVE *Rimonim*, cast and engraved silver, enamel, Morocco, 19th century

RIGHT Diadem for *tik*, cast and engraved silver, Algeria, 1913

OPPOSITE *Rimonim*, gilded, cast, engraved and pierced silver, Algeria, 1903

Me'il, velvet appliquéd with gold embroidery, Tangiers, 19th century

OPPOSITE ABOVE Drawing of a candelabrum from prayerbook shown below

OPPOSITE BELOW Two pages from a Sabbath prayerbook, hand-written and illustrated in colour, 'Song of the Sea' (Exodus 15) in arabesques, Turkey, 1815

Sabbath cloth, velvet embroidered in coloured wool, rituals connected with the meal, verses from the Torah and talmudic sayings are embroidered in circles, Persia, 19th century

The Sabbath

In addition to the regulations and laws governing the Sabbath, many maxims, legends and allegoric allusions have grown up around this seventh day, defined as a day of rest and sanctity: rest for the body, since all labour is forbidden, and sanctity for the spirit. When a man is liberated from his mundane cares and occupations, his mind is free to immerse itself in the Torah and in philosophical works, through which he can aspire to reach the nobility of the Sabbath and sense its holiness. Observance of this day is the fourth of the Ten Commandments, and the injunction to do so appears twice in the Torah: 'Remember the Sabbath day to keep it holy' (Exodus 20:8) and 'Keep the Sabbath day to sanctify it' (Deuteronomy 5:12). Jewish scholars have interpreted this repetition in different ways. Some said that the Sabbath candles are its glory and it is obligatory for the housewife to light at least two candles on Friday night: one for 'Remember' and one for 'Keep'; and if, for some reason, she has not lit the candles on one Sabbath, she must light an extra candle every Friday night for the rest of her life. There are some women who make it a practice to light an additional candle for each child that is born.

126

פרייטאג צו נאכט

בָּרוּךְ אַתָּה יי אֱלהֵינוּ מֶלֶךְ הָעוֹלָם אֲשֶׁר קִדְשָׁנוּ בְּמִצְוֹתָיו
וְצִוָּנוּ לְהַדְלִיק נֵר שֶׁל שַׁבָּת

Special prayers have been written for the kindling of the Sabbath lights, and the custom is for the Jewish woman to cover her eyes with her hands while concentrating on a widespread prayer for the welfare of her family. Artists have found inspiration in the figure of the mother lighting the Sabbath candles and have given creative expression to this religious, emotional experience.

Other Sabbath customs have offered artists and craftsmen rich stimuli for their imaginations, and they have created beautiful utensils for the day, including silver, brass, glass and ivory candlesticks and candelabra; silver beakers for wine; containers for salt and even tobacco cases specially inscribed for the Sabbath.

As it was customary in ancient times to welcome the Sabbath with branches of myrtle, so during the service to usher out the Sabbath – the *havdallah* – people inhaled the fragrances of their branches. When the *Mavdil* prayer distinguishing 'between holy and ordinary, between light and darkness' was recited, myrtle was passed from hand to hand. In the course of generations aromatic spices began to replace the myrtle, but long usage has preserved the name 'myrtle' (*hadass*) for the spice box.

The use of sweet-smelling herbs and spices roused the creative instincts of artisans and they fashioned spice boxes in widely varied designs and

Kindling the Sabbath lights, woodcut from a book of customs, Amsterdam, 1723

Hanging Sabbath lamp, cast, hammered, engraved and partially gilded silver, with six branches, Poland, 1848

OPPOSITE (clockwise) Candlestick, cast, hammered, engraved and partially gilded silver, Poland, 18th century; oil lamp, pierced, engraved and hammered silver, Morocco, 19th century; oil lamp shaped like a bowl, engraved, partially gilded silver, Persia, 1834; earthenware oil lamp, seven apertures, ornamentation in form of olive leaf, Gerasa excavations, 2nd century

Pair of candle holders, hammered, partially gilded silver, letters on base are Kabbalistic combination alluding to the name of God, Austria, 18th century

BELOW Tobacco box for the Sabbath, engraved and hammered silver, Tunisia, 19th century

Cloth for covering the Sabbath loaf, print on cloth depicting Montefiore's coat of arms, utensils of the Temple, the Western Wall, Rachel's Tomb and David's Tower, Jerusalem, 1871

ABOVE Page with Sabbath ordinances, from a drawn and illustrated parchment manuscript, Germany, 1313

LEFT Wine goblets for Sabbath benediction (*kiddush*) (from left): engraved silver adorned with scales and inscription, Poland, 18th century; cast and engraved silver with lid and bird, India, 18th century; engraved, gilded silver showing Rachel's Tomb and the Western Wall, Poland, 19th century

LEFT Spice box, pierced and engraved silver shaped like a tower, Nuremberg, 18th century

RIGHT Spice box, pierced and engraved silver, Poland, 19th century

LEFT Containers for embers and aromatic seeds, engraved, hammered, cast and gilded silver, 16th–17th century

RIGHT Spice box shaped like a pine cone, engraved and carved silver, Poland

Silver spice boxes for *havdalah* (from left): in shape of poppy on stem, Poland, 18th century; in shape of sunflower, Poland, 18th century; in shape of fish, Poland, 18th century; in shape of fruit on a single stem. Poland, 18th century; in shape of fruit with squirrel, Poland, 18th century; (centre) plate for *havdalah* ceremony, engraved pewter, Germany, 1822

shapes in gold, silver, brass, glass and wood. In Ashkenazi circles, architectural figures, such as towers surrounded by pennants and bells, were very popular forms for these containers. As a rule, these are made of silver filigree or repoussé, some with a clock on the façade indicating the hour of the Sabbath's departure. Since the source of inspiration was the tower in the mediaeval city, the spire is sometimes surrounded by an open balcony with miniature replicas of armed guards on duty at each corner or figures representing outstanding functionaries of the Jewish community: the rabbi, the ritual slaughterer, the cantor and the beadle. There are also more intricate containers used both for spices and for the candles that mark the Sabbath's end, or a goblet with a perforated lid to permit the aroma to escape. The fragrance of the spices suggested the shapes of flowers or aromatic fruits, and artists created boxes resembling roses, poppies, sunflowers, citrons, pears and pomegranates, while some gave their fancy free rein in creating beautiful imaginative forms.

OPPOSITE Spice boxes (from left): tower, cast and filigreed silver with figures of four guards, Germany, 18th century; high tower, engraved and filigreed silver, Poland, 18th century; steam engine, filigreed and cast silver, Austria, 19th century; tower with clock, engraved silver, Germany, 18th century; wine goblet, hammered and engraved silver, Germany, 18th century

Spice box, filigreed silver set with precious stones and eight enamel miniatures of biblical scenes, Western Europe, 18th century

LEFT Illustrated page of a prayer for the new moon, Persia, 1904

BELOW Sanctification of the new moon, woodcut from a book of customs, Amsterdam, 1723

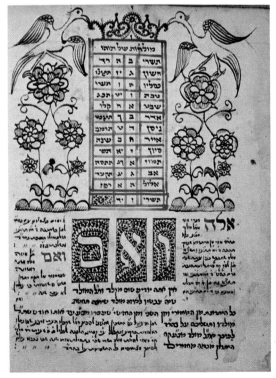

ABOVE Blessing the new moon, etching from a book by J.C. Bodenschatz, 1748

LEFT List of the months, illustrated page from the book *Evronot*, Poland, 1640

The First of the Month

The Hebrew month, which is based on the lunar calendar, begins with the appearance of the new moon. To the Jews of antiquity, the first of the month was an important date, and the Torah speaks of it as one of the holidays: 'Also in the day of your gladness, and in your solemn days, and in the beginnings of your months, ye shall blow the trumpets [*shofar*]. . . .' (Numbers 10:10). In the wilderness the *shofar* was used to call the people together and signal that the time had come to break camp and move on; in the Temple the *shofar* counted among the musical instruments. During times of war they were used to sound the alarm and for battle orders, which is why the ram's horn, of which the *shofar* is made, appears on the coins Bar-Kokhba issued in the year 134 CE during his war against the Romans.

During the Second Temple period and for a time thereafter, the first of the month was determined by the evidence of witnesses who came before the Sanhedrin and testified that they had seen the new moon. There were two ways in which the announcement of the new moon was transmitted: torches were lit on mountain tops, and runners were sent from the Land of Israel to distant places, so that the people in the Diaspora would know the proper date for celebrating the holidays and festivals, as the Torah indicates the day of the month on which these occasions fall. The astronomical calculation of the Hebrew calendar was finally fixed by Hillel Ha-Nasi, apparently in the year 359 CE, and we still abide by it today.

Each month has its constellation, one of the signs of the zodiac (a Mesopotamian system for divination that was spread westward and modified by the Hellenists). In ancient Jewish literature, too, the names of the constellations and their courses are mentioned, but divination by the stars and the signs of the zodiac is absolutely forbidden by the Torah injunction: 'Neither shall ye use enchantments' (Leviticus 19:26). In the Middle Ages some of the Jewish scholars showed a tendency to believe in the influence of the horoscope on a man's destiny, in predetermining the good or ill that would befall him, but moralists refuted this view. The signs of the zodiac play an important role as allegoric and decorative motifs in Jewish art and literature. They appear in friezes, mosaic floors of ancient synagogues and in wall and ceiling paintings in later synagogues. They are also used by the authors of books on astronomy and by the editors of the Hebrew calendar; they even appear in the prayerbooks and on the *mapot* that were dedicated to the *sifrei Torah*.

Upon seeing the new moon a special benediction instituted by the talmudic sages is recited with reference to the waxing and the waning. The moon is blessed under the open sky by the congregation, and they conclude with the words: 'David, King of Israel lives forever.'

A *dinar* (coin) from the time of Bar-Kokhba, silver, showing two rams' horns surrounded by the inscription: 'To the freedom of Jerusalem', Jerusalem, 134 CE

The New Year and the Day of Atonement

Ancient Jewish sources give two dates as the beginning of the new year: the month of Nissan (in the spring) and the month of Tishri, the seventh month (in the autumn). Nissan is the month of leafing and blossoming, Tishri the time of a man's spiritual renewal following the ten days known as the 'Days of Awe', which are devoted to prayer and penitence and conclude with a twenty-four-hour fast, the Day of Atonement, a time when a man's deeds are weighed and his fate for the coming year determined accordingly. The sounding of the *shofar* has a central place in the New Year prayer sequence. Jewish tradition has transmitted the belief that the first of Tishri is the day on which the world was created (and that Isaac was to be sacrificed) and it is in commemoration of the event that the *shofar* is sounded repeatedly during the prayer reading.

ABOVE Sounding the *shofar*, woodcut from a book of customs, Amsterdam, 1723

ABOVE RIGHT The sacrifice of Isaac, woodcut from the *Tzena Urena*, Amsterdam, 1766

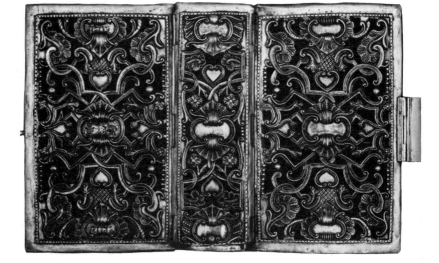

RIGHT Prayerbook binding, pierced, hammered and engraved silver, cartouche shows the sacrifice of Isaac, Germany, 18th century

138

Etching by Rembrandt of the
sacrifice of Isaac, Holland, 17th
century

In Tonagefimonono etatis abrahe aïo apparuit ei deus ⁊ pmiſit ǫ filius de ſara vxoɫe naſceref quē yſaac vocari iuſſit. Cūǫ yſaac ǫnǫ ⁊ .xx. eſſet annoɫ voles deus abrahe obedientiā pɫobare:ipm filiū ſibi imolari pɫecepit. Qui repente dei iuſſa adimplere ſtuduit. Et cū ad cedem filij pariter ⁊ ad altare acceſſ ſiſſet. deus cognita hois obedientia clamauit. abrahā ne extēdas manū in puerū. nūc cognoui ǫ timeas do minū. Et cōſeſtim arietē ex ipɫouiſo vepɫibꝰ inherētē ad ſacrificiū pɫtulit. Cū abɫahā obediſſet dño in ymo latione filij ſui yſaac. facta eſt ad eū dulcis illa repɫomiſſio de chɫiſto dicente ſibi deo. In ſemine tuo benedi centur omnes gentes. quia obediſti voci mee.

ABOVE 'The Sacrifice of Isaac', coloured woodcut, Nuremberg, 1493

LEFT Buckle of belt for the *kitel* showing the sacrifice of Isaac and signs of the zodiac, Galicia (Austria), 1817

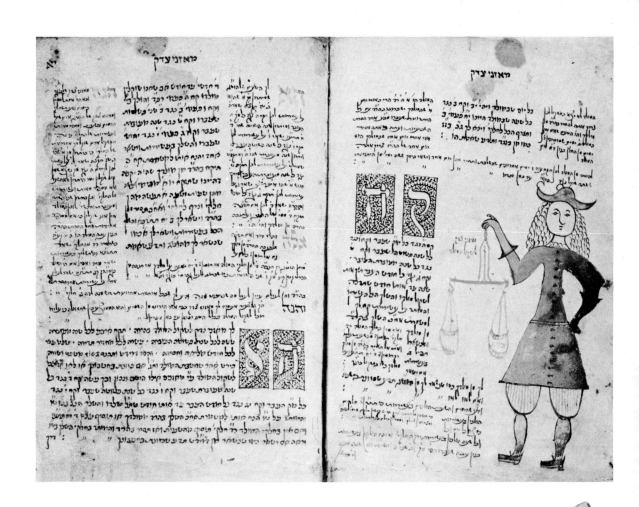

ABOVE Page for the month of Elul from the book *Evronot*, zodiac sign of the month is a virgin holding scales, symbol of the Day of Judgement, Poland, 1640

RIGHT *Shofar* with decorative engraving and verses from the Torah, Europe, 19th century

BELOW *Shofar*, Yemen, 19th century

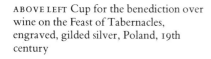

ABOVE LEFT Cup for the benediction over wine on the Feast of Tabernacles, engraved, gilded silver, Poland, 19th century

ABOVE RIGHT Cup for the benediction over wine on the Feast of Tabernacles, hammered, engraved and gilded silver, Germany, 18th century

RIGHT (from left) Citron box, coconut shell and engraved silver, Austria, 1816; citron box, coconut shell, silver decoration, Vienna, 1800; bowl for citron, engraved, hammered, gilded silver, Germany, 17th–18th century; (below) sheath for myrtles that were used together with palm branches on the festival and for *havdalah* spice, plaited silver, Palestine, 20th century

The Feast of Tabernacles

The Feast of Tabernacles is one of the three major holidays during which the Israelites made a pilgrimage to the Temple in Jerusalem. The holiday, which lasts for seven days, is characterized primarily by two acts: dwelling in booths (*sukkot*) and waving the palm branch. The booths commemorate the time when the Israelites wandered in the wilderness and lived in tents and booths; the decorated palm branch symbolizes the era of freedom and prosperity in the Land of Israel, when the Jews' prime source of livelihood was agriculture. During the holiday the celebrants hold a cluster of four kinds of vegetation enumerated in the Torah: a citrus (*etrog*), palm branches (*lulav*), the boughs of thick trees (myrtle) and willows of the brook. The three branches are tied together and a benediction is recited over them and the citron. On the eighth day of the festival Jews do not dwell in the booths, and, according to the Bible, this is a holiday unto itself – 'The Eighth Day, an Assembly' (*Shmini Atzeret*). It is then that the water allocation and the agricultural yield are determined and a special prayer is recited asking that rain be timely and drought prevented. In Israel this same day is also known as Rejoicing in the Law (Simhat Torah) and marks the completion of the annual cycle of reading from the Torah, while in the Diaspora the two occasions are celebrated on separate days. On the eve of the day of Simhat Torah, the congregation encircles the platform in song and dance, bearing in their arms all the *sifrei Torah* the synagogue possesses.

Citron box, engraved pewter, Holland, 18th century

Citron box in shape of citron, engraved, gilded silver, Russia, 18th century

Prayers in the synagogue on the Feast of Tabernacles, coloured etching, London, 1800

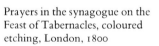

Prayers in synagogue on the Feast of Tabernacles, cast copper relief by M. Farbman

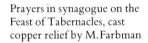

OPPOSITE *Parochet* for *aron ha-kodesh* on Feast of Tabernacles, silver and gold embroidery on velvet, inscription: 'Ye shall dwell in booths seven days', the Western Wall and Solomon's Temple, Turkey, 19th century

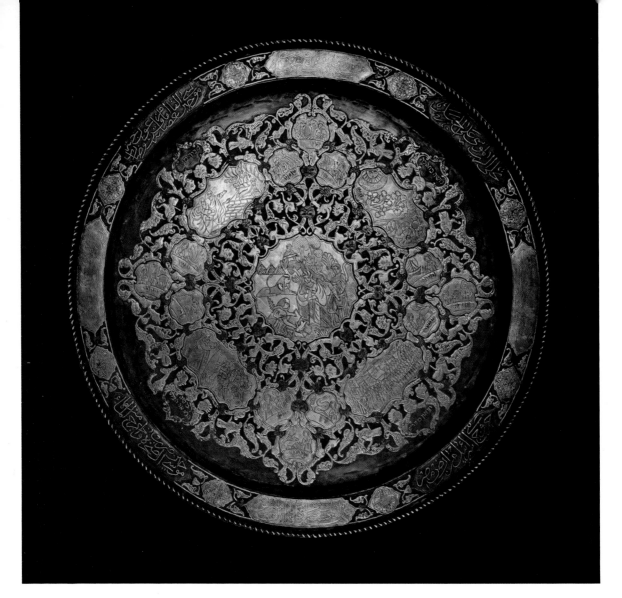

Passover

Seder plate, gold, silver and bronze set in copper, showing symbols of the tribes and depiction of the Exodus from Egypt with explanation in Hebrew and Arabic, Baghdad, 20th century

Passover, also called the Festival of Unleavened Bread (*matzot*), falls on the fifteenth day of the month of Nissan and is celebrated for seven days. In the era of the Temple, the Israelites made pilgrimages to Jerusalem in multitudes to celebrate the holiday and fulfil the commandment to sacrifice the paschal lamb on the proper date. The festival commemorates the most remarkable historic event in Israel's past, the miracle of the Exodus from Egypt in the thirteenth century BCE, when the Israelites were redeemed from slavery and became a free people. Passover, therefore, is not a festival of nature or joy in material things but one of praise, an outstanding expression of the Jewish people's faith. It is also the only one of the holidays whose story the Torah enjoins the Jews to relate,

and the ancient sages decreed that 'It is praiseworthy to relate at length the story of the Exodus from Egypt.'

Passover is also the only festival for which the Torah sets down the food that may be eaten. An excess of tasty foods is prohibited and a variety of baked goods are not to be eaten. It is obligatory to eat the unleavened bread (*matzah*) made only with flour and water and no flavouring, not even salt. This is called the 'bread of affliction' and it is eaten with bitter herbs in memory of the period of bondage.

The most impressive and festive ceremony that takes place during Passover is the *seder*, held within the family circle on the first night of the holiday (and on the second night as well in the Diaspora). Candles are lit and the table is decorated with the most beautiful utensils and cutlery the family possesses. The story of the Exodus from Egypt is read from the Hagaddah, which was written between the second century BCE and the eighth century CE, a book that has appeared in more than 3,500 editions

Seder plate, glazed earthenware showing the *seder* table with the sanctification and the first words of the Hagaddah: 'This is the bread of affliction' encircling the plate, Hungary, 19th century

147

Seder plate, glazed earthenware
with symbols of the festival,
Jerusalem, 19th century

Case for *matzot*, embroidered
with fish scales and gold thread,
Hungary, 19th century

149

יהבוסים הללה

Facsimile of a page from the
Darmstadt Hagaddah,
Germany, 16th century

by now. The most important utensil at the *seder* is the Passover plate,
which is placed in front of the head of the family. Arranged in set order on
the plate are the *matzah*, bitter herbs, ground apples and spices
(*haroset*), an egg and a small piece of roast meat symbolizing the holiday
fare in the days of the Temple.

The *seder* arrangements and the utensils and appurtenances used for its
rituals have given rise to rich and fascinating artistic expression. From the
period of the Renaissance on, Passover plates were made of silver, pewter,
copper and ceramics. Envelopes for the three *matzot* were fashioned of
velvet, silk or fine linen, decorated with coloured embroidery, beads,
silver threads and fish scales. Other utensils were exquisitely wrought to
beautify the table on this festive night. Artists have made particular efforts
to beautify the Hagaddah with colourful illustrations, block prints and
copper engravings.

OPPOSITE Passover goblet,
carved ivory with inscription:
'Let my people go', Moses and
Aaron in front of Pharaoh,
Germany, 18th century

(clockwise) Wine flagon, glass, Bohemia, 19th century; wine goblet, handle in shape of wing, engraved cast silver inscribed 'Passover cup', Russia, 19th century; Passover plate, china, England, 19th century; Elijah's cup, hammered, engraved silver inscribed 'Elijah's cup', England, 19th century; vessel for *haroset*, gilded, engraved silver, Germany, 19th century; *seder* plate, engraved, hammered silver with family emblems and inscription: 'And I will take you to me for a people' (Exodus 7:7), Italy, 17th–18th century

'The Seder', aquatint etching, France

RIGHT Portrait of R. Shlomo Ben Zvi, head of the rabbinical court of the London Ashkenazi community, who translated the Hagaddah into English

FOR THE

TWO FIRST NIGHTS

OF

PASSOVER;

IN HEBREW AND ENGLISH.

ACCORDING TO THE CUSTOM OF THE

GERMAN AND POLISH JEWS.

CAREFULLY REVISED AND CORRECTED,

By ISAAC LEVI,

TEACHER OF THE HEBREW LANGUAGE, &c.

London:

Printed and Sold by E. Justins, 54, Brick Lane, Spitalfields.

PUBLISHED BY HYAM BARNETT, HEBREW BOOKSELLER, ADAM'S COURT, NEW COURT, DUKE'S PLACE; AND I. JOSEPH, SAM'S COFFEE-HOUSE, DUKE'S PLACE.

A. M. 5568.

FAR RIGHT Passover Hagaddah with English translation, London, 1789

Buckle for *kitel* worn on Passover and the Day of Atonement, with symbols appropriate for both, engraved silver, Lublin, 1821

Seder plate, engraved pewter
with a two-headed eagle,
emblem of the Hapsburg
empire, and gilt letters J II
(Joseph II, emperor of Austria)

Seder plate, engraved pewter
with symbols of the festival,
Germany, 1790

Hanukkah

Hanukkah, a holiday lasting eight days, begins on the twenty-fifth of Kislev, the ninth month of the Hebrew calendar. It is an ancient religious-national holiday in character and origin and is still celebrated in the manner instituted by the talmudic rabbis. The historic background of the holiday is the victory of the Jews over the Seleucid Greeks following the long struggle against the cruel reign of Antiochus Epiphanes, who proscribed the laws of the Torah. Antiochus stole from the Temple the golden seven-branched candelabrum – the distinguishing symbol of Israel from the time of Moses – and his armies maliciously defiled all the consecrated oil to prevent the Jews from fulfilling the command to kindle the lamp with that oil only. When the Hasmoneans prevailed over the Seleucids and the Maccabean army entered Jerusalem, its commanding officer, Judah the Maccabee, nullified the edicts of Antiochus and reinstated the laws of the Torah.

Judah began to repair the Temple and rid it of the pagan statuary and symbols with which the Greeks had sullied it. To replace the stolen candelabrum, the Jews made a temporary one out of iron spokes, apparently salvaged from their primitive weapons of war. Thus they were able to renew services in the Temple, but still there was no pure oil. Suddenly they discovered a clay jug closed with the seal of the High Priest, and in it was enough oil for one night. On the twenty-fifth of Kislev in the year 164 BCE the Jews of Jerusalem celebrated the dedication of the Temple and kindled the seven-branched candelabrum. To spread the news of the victory, lights were also kindled in all the yards of Jerusalem, and the celebration was called Hanukkah (which means dedication). The well-known legend goes on to tell that although the lamp burned in the Temple throughout the night, no oil was consumed and the cups remained full. This miracle was repeated for eight days, until pure oil was brought from outside the city.

The memory of the victory over Antiochus' army is celebrated not by gay processions and elaborate feasting but by lighting a modest candle in every Jewish home, one on the first night of the holiday and an additional one each succeeding night, until eight candles are burning. The importance of the Hanukkah lamp in the Jewish home spurred Jewish

Tops for a Hanukkah game: (above) silver filigree, Holland, 19th century; (below) ivory, Russia

BELOW Hanukkah lamp shaped like chairs, cast lead, Germany, 19th century

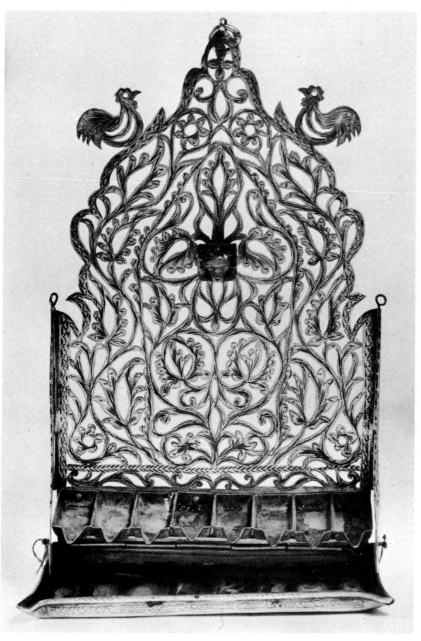

Hanukkah lamp, pierced, engraved silver with basin for drippings, Morocco, 20th century

LEFT Hanukkah lamp, brass, India, 19th century

RIGHT Hanukkah lamp, partially gilded, pierced, engraved silver with dedicatory inscription, North Africa, 1933

157

ABOVE Hanukkah lamp, hammered and engraved brass, Holland, 17th century

BELOW Hanukkah lamp, cast bronze, Carpentras, France, 16th century

ABOVE Hanukkah lamp, pierced and hammered brass, Holland, 18th century

BELOW Hanukkah lamp, cast bronze, Sicily, 17th–18th century

OPPOSITE ABOVE Hanukkah lamp, glazed earthenware shaped like saucer, Slovakia, 1861

OPPOSITE LEFT Hanukkah lamp, cast brass, Corfu, 1871

OPPOSITE RIGHT Hanukkah lamp, cast bronze in shape of wooden synagogue with holders for Sabbath candles, Poland, 18th century

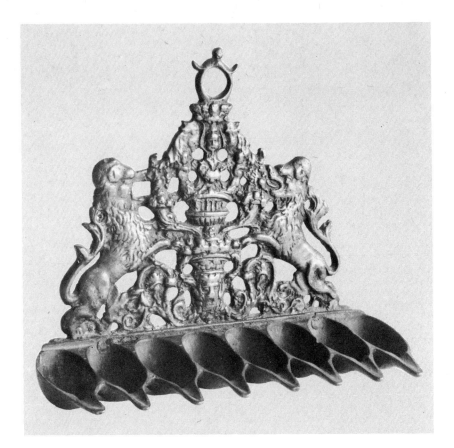

Hanukkah lamp, gilded cast bronze, Italy, 16th century

LEFT Hanukkah lamp, hammered, engraved silver, Italy, 18th century

RIGHT Hanukkah lamp, engraved cast bronze, Italy, 1623

LEFT Hanukkah lamp, gilded cast brass, Prague, 18th century

RIGHT Hanukkah lamp, cast, pierced and hammered silver, Frankfurt on Main, 1744

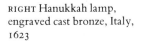

160

ABOVE Hanukkah lamp, cast, filigreed silver with holders for Sabbath candles, Ukraine, 18th century

LEFT Hanukkah lamp, engraved and hammered silver with inscription: 'Kindle the Hanukkah light', Poland, 18th century

RIGHT Hanukkah lamp, engraved copper, Damascus, 19th century

artists to create such lamps of silver, copper, brass, pewter, glass, ceramics and wood and to execute them in interesting and variegated shapes. The Hanukkah lights are invested with holiness, as they proclaim a miracle of antiquity. Early sages therefore ordained that their light was not to be used for ordinary purposes. As illumination in the home was by candle-light until the advent of electricity, alongside each Hanukkah lamp the sages instituted the use of a special candle for normal household purposes, calling it the 'caretaker' (*shamash*). It is in memory of this tradition that we continue to light the extra candle today.

Hanukkah lamp, combination of copper and silver frets with brass, depicting the Temple site, Western Wall and Ten Commandments with biblical verses, Damascus synagogue, 20th century

Hanukkah lamp, engraved, pierced and hammered silver, *shamash* on a rosette at height of crossbar, North Africa, 19th century

Hanukkah lamp, pierced and hammered brass, Tunisia, 19th century

Hanukkah lamp, soft stone shaped like a flower with engraved ornamentation, Persia, 19th century

Hanukkah lamp, cast brass and glass, India, 18th century

Purim

Purim falls on the fourteenth and fifteenth days of the month of Adar, the twelfth month of the year. As it is not included among the 'holy convocations', there is no ban on work during this holiday, unless the public in a given place takes it upon itself to refrain from following normal occupations. The historic background of Purim is associated with a scheme devised by Haman, a minister in the royal court of Persia during the reign of King Xerxes, who connived against Mordechai the Jew, a descendant of King Saul. Haman plotted to destroy not only Mordechai but all the Jews as well, 'young and old, children and women, in one day ... and to take the spoil of them for a prey'. He chose the date of this total destruction by casting lots (*purim* in Hebrew). After the minister had deposited 10,000 talents of silver in the treasury, the king affixed his signature to the decree Haman had prepared, and plans were made to put it into effect.

The story of these events and of the salvation of the community are recorded in the Scroll of Esther, which is read to the congregation in the synagogue on the eve and the morning of Purim. In memory of the danger that threatened Persian Jewry and of its deliverance, two days are celebrated in joyous drinking and feasting, and people send portions (*manot*) of home-made delicacies to their friends and gifts to the poor.

Inspired by the customs that have become part of this holiday, artists have created a variety of decorative utensils. Their major efforts, however, have been concentrated on the text of the scroll, which has been illustrated and embellished in widely varying styles and techniques: painting, etching, cutouts and so forth. Handsome sheaths of silver, ivory and olive wood have also been wrought for the scroll.

Form for baking Purim cakes, carved wood depicting two fish (zodiac sign for the month of Adar) and a goblet, Central Europe, 19th century

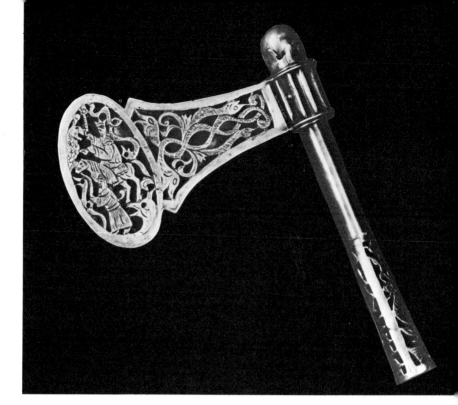

Rattle, engraved and pierced
silver with scenes from the
Purim story and Torah, birds
and flowers on handle, United
States, 20th century

Plate for sending Purim
portions, engraved, hammered
silver, Germany, 19th century

ויהי בימי אחשורו
מהדו ועד כוש שב
בימים ההם כשבת
מלכותו אשר בשו
למלכו עשה משתה
ומדי הפרתמים וש
את עשר כבוד מל
ימים רבים שמונים
האלה עשה המלך
הבירה למגדול וע
בחצר גנת ביתן ה
אחוז בחבלי בוץ ו
שש מטות זהב וכ
וסחרת והשקות בכ
ויין מלכות רב כיד
כי כן יסד המלך ש
איש ואיש
משתה נשים בית

Esther scroll on parchment, hand-written
with copper etching in margins, wooden
case, Prague, 18th century

OPPOSITE Esther scroll on parchment in
silver case, niello illustrations and name of
owner on clasp, Balkans, 1903

167

Case for Esther scroll, engraved and hammered silver,
Europe, 19th century

OPPOSITE Cases for Esther scrolls (from left): parchment,
carved-wood handle, Yemen, 18th century; parchment,
pierced and carved ivory handle, Turkey, 19th century;
cast, engraved, gilded silver decorated with amber, Iraq,
19th century; cast, filigreed, gilded silver with amber,
Morocco, 19th century; parchment rolled on engraved and
carved wooden handle, Persia, 19th century; gilded,
filigreed silver with precious stones, Turkey, 18th century

OPPOSITE ABOVE Esther scroll on parchment, carved
wooden handle, silver adornments and bone buttons,
Persia, opening picture and decorative drawings repeated
throughout scrolls, 19th–20th century

OPPOSITE BELOW Esther scroll, repetition of coloured
sketch of Oriental gates, Persia, 19th century

BELOW Esther scroll, parchment on silver handle,
Italy, 18th century

BOTTOM Esther scroll, parchment rolled on wood,
Morocco, 19th century

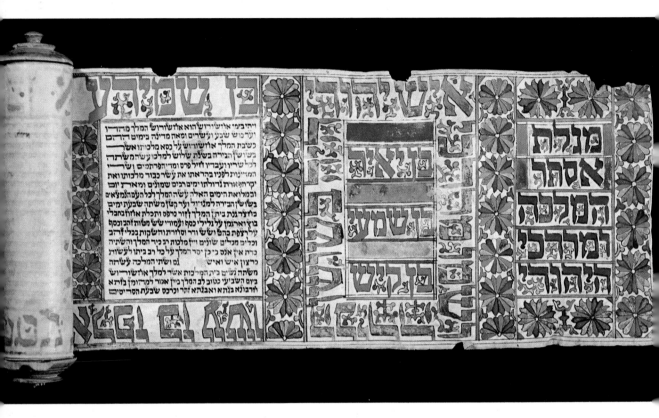

Esther scroll, decorated
parchment rolled on wood,
Mordechai's genealogy traced
back to Abraham, Haman's to
Esau, Morocco, 19th century

Cases for Esther scroll: (above) engraved and hammered silver, Casablanca, 19th century; (below) engraved silver shaped like rattle, scroll of micrographic script, dedicatory inscription, Palestine, 19th century

Esther scroll, parchment,
carved-wood handle, Lisbon, 1816

Esther scroll, parchment,
Holland, 18th century

RIGHT Memorial plaque to deceased woman, hammered, gilded silver, Morocco, 1917

BELOW RIGHT Alms box, engraved silver, shaped like tombstone and grave with inscription: 'Righteousness delivereth from death' and dedicatory inscription, Burgenland, 1825

BELOW Alms box, hammered tin and iron, Germany, 17th–18th century

The House of Life

Jews refer to the cemetery as 'the house of life' in association with the biblical passage: 'May the soul of my master be bound up in the bonds of life with the Lord', and the first letters of this prayer in Hebrew are engraved on tombstones. For some 2,000 years every Jewish settlement has had a burial society. Its members voluntarily assume the task of burying the dead, and they thereby relieve the mourners of a duty that involves great suffering and emotional distress. In a traditional environment it is considered an honour to be a member of the burial society, and the leading figures and outstanding personalities of the community belong to it. In some places an ancient ordinance limits the number of society members to eighteen, a number associated in Hebrew with life.

Throughout the centuries a specific art has grown up around the fashioning of the tombstones. They are cut in stone, sculptured or cast, and a set of appropriate symbols and inscriptions has evolved. Boxes of silver, brass or tin bearing the inscription 'Charity saves from death' are also examples of interesting workmanship. These are used during the funeral and at the actual interment, and the money deposited in them is primarily to assist impoverished bereaved families.

Parallel with the belief in the coming of the Messiah, Jewry believes in the resurrection of the dead as one of the thirteen principles of its faith. This belief has been rooted deeply in Israel since earliest times and finds expression in visions of the prophets, such as Ezekiel's vision of the resurrection of the dried bones and in the 'Song of Hannah': 'The Lord killeth and maketh alive: he bringeth down to the grave, and bringeth up' (1 Samuel 2:6), or in the vision of Daniel: 'And many of them that sleep in the dust of the earth shall awake' (Daniel 12:2). In certain verses of the scriptures, Jewish scholars have perceived allegorical allusions to resurrection in references to plants: 'And the Lord . . . shall guide thee continually, and satisfy thy soul in drought and make thy bones fat; and thou shalt be like a watered garden' (Isaiah 58:11). Such allusions have influenced Jewish artisans to use the forms of natural vegetation to symbolize the concept of resurrection of the dead on gravestones and on ritual utensils and vessels.

View of old cemetery in Prague, etching by H. Stainer-Prage, 20th century

Photograph of prayerbook, script in colour and ornamented, Turkey, 1815

Poem '*Yigdal*' written in 15th century and based on the thirteen principles of the Jewish faith

OPPOSITE Tombstone in Prague cemetery with plant symbolizing the resurrection of the dead

Glossary

ARON HA-KODESH, the beautiful receptacle for the *sefer Torah* in modern synagogues (called the Ark of the Torah, a reference to the ark from the time of Moses). In the Bible it is called the Ark of the Covenant or the Ark of the Testimony and is referred to only once as the Ark of the Torah (II Chronicles 38:3). The original ark vanished when the First Temple was destroyed in 586 BCE and it was never duplicated or replaced. When the Second Temple was built, the place of the ark in the Tabernacle remained empty, although all the rites of the Day of Atonement were carried out in accordance with the biblical instructions. In the synagogues that were built in the Land of Israel after the destruction of the Second Temple (70 CE), no permanent closed place was set aside for the *sefer Torah* because of the people's desire to refrain from investing the synagogue with the attributes of the Temple, whether in architectural form or in interior furnishings. The *sifrei Torah* were not kept inside the synagogue but in a nearby dwelling or behind a curtain adjacent to the hall of prayer. In those days a movable rectangular box – called an *aron* (closet) in Hebrew and an *arona* in Aramaic (Jerusalem Talmud, Mishna, Taanit 2) – was used for this purpose. When the box containing the *sefer Torah* was brought into the synagogue for the obligatory reading, it was placed facing the worshippers, with its back towards Jerusalem.

The *aron ha-kodesh* in its contemporary upright form is the result of some 2,000 years of continuous artistic, geographic and historic influences in which folk tradition and functional adaptations merged. At first it was an open apse formed in the inner wall of the synagogue that faced Jerusalem, to indicate the direction of prayer, and it was not intended for the *sifrei Torah*. An excellent example is the domed apse in the third-century CE synagogue that was discovered at Dura Europos on the Euphrates River in Syria. The inside of the apse was decorated with coloured frescoes in geometric patterns, and at its head was a jutting architectural shell reminiscent of the entrance gate to the Second Temple. The *aron ha-kodesh* was apparently fixed in a permanent place in the hall of prayer in about the eighth century, but we have no definite material, either tangible or literary, to enable us to describe its form. Jewish sources call the box in which the *sefer Torah* was kept a 'modest container' (Taanit 16–1). Hence the mosaic representations of the box cannot be considered to reflect its structure, for had such a splendid receptacle been visible to the worshippers in the synagogue, what need was there to depict it on the mosaic floor? It is reasonable to assume that under the influence of the commentaries of certain sages, the artists of that era created an imaginative reproduction of the closed Temple doors. These, together with the holy vessels around them, inspired the public to pray for the reconstruction of the Temple, a hope which still finds expression in prayers recited in the synagogue today.

The forms on the gilded windows and on tombstones in the Jewish catacombs in Rome are also apparently not the *aron ha-kodesh* but depictions of a closet in a private home, referred to in the Talmud as a *migdal* (tower), with shelves for scrolls (Megilla 3, 1). It was customary in Eastern Europe to carve an open bookcase with shelves containing rows of books on the tombstones of scholars and rabbis. Inspiration for this theme is found in the verse: 'When thou sleepest it shall keep thee; and when thou awakest, it shall talk with thee' (Proverbs 6:22), interpreted by the sages as a reference to death and the resurrection of the dead.

The transition from a simple rectangular box to a splendid upright cabinet took place over a long period. The cabinet evolved from the symbolic apse through the case and tower and was influenced by the upright cabinets for holy books that developed in the surrounding societies. There was, however, a basic and definitive difference between these cabinets and the *aron ha-kodesh* in that the latter has no shelves and the *sifrei Torah* stand upright within it. Traditionally the *sefer Torah* was placed at the side of the *aron ha-kodesh* to conform to the biblical description: 'Moses commanded the Levites, which bare the Ark of the Covenant of the Lord, saying, Take this book of the law and put it in the side of the Ark of the Covenant of the Lord your God, that it may be there for a witness against thee' (Deuteronomy 31:25).

Great artistic richness, vision and imagination have been invested by Jewish artists in designing the *aron ha-kodesh*, and this specialized artistic field developed steadily through the Renaissance, Baroque and Rococo periods and later; it is still expanding and acquiring new, modern forms consonant with the taste and influences prevalent in various countries.

Artists exercise sweeping creative initiative in this sphere, and no two arks are alike. To the Jewish craftsman, planning and producing an *aron ha-kodesh* is a spiritually moving and sanctified task that fills him with creative joy.

SEFER TORAH (plural SIFREI TORAH), the Torah scroll from which passages are read aloud, is the holiest object in the synagogue. It imbues the entire building with sanctity, and all the utensils and adornments connected with the scroll are called 'holy vessels'. The *sefer Torah* contains the five books of the Pentateuch copied in sequence by an expert scribe on sheets of parchment made of the specially processed skin of ritually clean animals. The scribe is forbidden to write even a single letter from memory, but must copy letter for letter from a perfect book, proofread by a method that has been passed on from generation to generation for thousands of years. Three approved and proofread scrolls were preserved in the court of the Second Temple, and the scribes proofread their work against them. Regulations and customs were codified in ancient times not only to ensure the accuracy of the original text of the Bible, but also to invest it with an attractive form that was uniform, symmetrical and aesthetically pleasing.

The *sefer Torah* is not written with a metal or even a gold pen but with a quill or reed; it may not be written in script for each letter must be separate. In accordance with a fixed tradition, the letters are straight and printed in black ink only, without punctuation, vowel sounds or any adornment whatsoever; the only exception is a modest design in the form of small crowns above seven specifically chosen letters. A set number of lines appears on each page, no fewer than forty-two and no more than sixty, each containing thirty letters.

According to the tradition established by the scribes in Jerusalem in the third century CE, the scroll is rolled on two poles from its ends until the poles meet in the middle. These poles are called 'trees of life' after the verse: 'It is a tree of life to them that lay hold upon it' (Proverbs 3:18). An ancient traditional law obliges every Jew to write a *sefer Torah* for himself, and if he does not know how he must buy one with his own money. While the Temple stood, multitudes would come to its court on the Day of Atonement to hear the High Priest's reading, and each man brought his own scroll to display its beauty. In our own times, Ashkenazi Jews read from the *sefer Torah* while it rests on the reader's table on the synagogue platform, while the Oriental communities let it stand in its *tik*. In the early synagogues the reader would hold the open scroll with both hands, as shown in one of the Dura Europos paintings.

TIK (plural TIKIM), a sheath or case that was made of wood or leather in the talmudic era and held various articles, such as musical instruments, writing implements, and so forth, as well as the *sefer Torah*. Among the Oriental communities (as well as the Samaritans) it is still customary to follow the tradition that began in the sixteenth century under the architectonic influence of Spain: they fashion a separate *tik* for each scroll, which is not usually the practice in the Ashkenazi communities. Today *tikim* are made of wood or silver in cylindrical form with the two halves hinged. The *sefer Torah* is taken from the *aron ha-kodesh* in its *tik* and placed on the platform in an upright position for the reading. *Tikim* are made of carved wood and of gilded silver, decorated with symbols, geometric forms and dedications, whorls and corals.

MAPAH (plural MAPOT), a long cloth binding (called in the sources a *mapah* if it is up to 20 cm wide and a *mitpachat* if it is wider and covers the entire height of the scroll) in which the *sefer Torah* is bound after the reading. The *mapah* is symbolic of the 'belt' worn by the Temple's High Priest, which was made of a colourful woven material and embellished with representations of the lion and the eagle. The Mishna (a collection of the oral law compiled in the first to second centuries CE) mentions decorated and embroidered *mapot* and *mitpachot* intended for the *sifrei Torah*, and special artists responsible for preparing them worked in the home of R. Judah Ha-Nasi, the editor of the Mishna. Influenced by the descriptions of the belt in the Torah and the Talmud, Jewish women in later ages embroidered their names and the names of members of their family on *mapot* presented to the synagogue in honour of special family occasions.

From the sixteenth century on, an interesting custom took root among

German Jewry and spread to other countries as well. They cut the cloth that swaddled an infant after his circumcision into strips and fashioned it into a binder for the *sefer Torah* called a *Wimpel* (in German). The connection between the swaddling cloth and the *sefer Torah* may well be questioned. The custom derives from an interesting incident that occurred at the beginning of the fifteenth century in the city of Mainz. A child was circumcised and the city's rabbi, the well-known sage R. Ya'akov Segal Moellin (the Maharil) was the godfather. As the ritual began, the congregants found that no swaddling cloth had been prepared, and the rabbi ordered that a *mapah* be taken from the *sefer Torah* to wrap around the child's legs. He stated that for this purpose it was permissible to use even a page of the *sefer Torah* itself, as a life was in danger. When the rabbi was asked whether the *mapah* should be returned to the scroll, he decreed only that it be laundered and the blood removed, and that its sanctity had not been affected. He added that the family should donate something to the synagogue so that they would not enjoy its benefits free of charge. Thus the art of adorning the *Wimpel* evolved from the decision of a most recognized authority in matters of law and tradition.

PAROCHET (plural PAROCHOT), the beautiful curtain that hangs in front of the *aron ha-kodesh* in both Ashkenazi and Sephardi synagogues. The name is originally found in the description of the construction of the Tabernacle in the wilderness: 'And thou shalt make a veil [*parochet*] of blue, and purple, and scarlet and fine twined linen of cunning work' (Exodus 26:31). In the Tabernacle and the two Temples, the *parochet* separated the Holy of Holies from the rest of the building. From the descriptions in the Bible and Talmud, we learn that the *parochet* in the Tabernacle and in the First Temple had woven figures of cherubs flanked by a lion on one side and an eagle on the other. In the Second Temple, although the Holy of Holies contained no ark, a double *parochet* nonetheless separated the area from the rest of the Temple, and it was embroidered with plants, flowers and stars, as described in the writings of Joseph ben Mattathias (Josephus Flavius), himself a Temple priest.

There was a workshop in the vicinity of the Second Temple, and perhaps also of the First, where dozens of virgins engaged in artistic weaving and embroidery, for which they were paid out of public funds. Every year they would prepare two *parochot* for the Holy of Holies and a larger number (called 'curtains') for the entrances to the Temple. When the priests worshipped they would close the curtain over the entrance, and when they finished they drew it back. We find graphic testimony of this ritual in a fresco from the Dura Europos synagogue (now in the National Museum in Damascus with a replica in the museum of Yeshiva University, New York), where the curtain is drawn aside; in mosaics in Beth Shean dating from the sixth century, where the curtain covers the entrance; and at Hamath Tiberias, where it is bunched together in the form of a tie in the middle of the entrance.

In the talmudic period, when the *sefer Torah* was brought to the synagogue to be read, the box in which it was kept would be beautifully adorned with cloth, but when the *sefer Torah* was removed, the box would be divested of its adornment. This is the source of the custom of draping the *aron ha-kodesh* with a beautiful *parochet*. In the Oriental communities, it is customary to tie coloured scarves to the *tik* that contains the *sefer Torah*. Many *parochot* from the sixteenth century on have been preserved. They are made of splendid weaves, silk, velvet and brocade, and are adorned with letters and symbols embroidered in gold and silver; some are even embellished with pearls and gems.

CAPORET, a short curtain (lambrequin) hung over the *parochet* in Ashkenazi synagogues. The *caporet* is not mentioned in the Talmud in connection with the *sefer Torah*, and the name became generally accepted in association with the golden *caporet* that covered the Ark of the Covenant in the Tabernacle, although the modern *caporet* does not resemble it in either form or material. The *caporet*, like the *parochet*, is made of velvet and silk and is embroidered with representations of the Temple utensils, cherubs, *rimonim*, verses and dedications.

ME'IL (plural ME'ILIM), a wrapping for the *sefer Torah*, is likewise not mentioned in the Talmud or other ancient sources, for at the time the *sefer Torah* was wrapped in lengths of silk or linen. It is included for the first time as one of the 'holy vessels' in the early Middle Ages and is named after the outer robe worn by the High Priest, which was woven out of blue wool. The early *me'il*, shaped like the original robe, was narrow and closed at the top and wide and open at the bottom. This pattern was followed in Italy and Germany, while in Eastern Europe most of the *me'ilim* were shaped like a closed shirt, with two straps at the top to fit it over the two poles ('trees of life') on which the *sefer Torah* is rolled. The Yemenite community usually wrapped the *tik* containing the *sefer Torah* in a wide coloured kerchief, a kind of mantle that was tied at the top with a ribbon and adorned at the bottom with hollow silver buttons shaped like small bells. This is reminiscent of the High Priest's robe, which is described as having 'a golden bell and a pomegranate, upon the hem of the robe round about' (Exodus 28:34).

YAD L'TORAH, an instrument shaped like a rod or baton, now called a *yad* (hand) because the tip of the rod is shaped like a hand with an extended finger. The reader of the Torah in the synagogue uses the *yad* to avoid touching the parchment but primarily in order to keep from skipping lines and reciting from memory, because according to traditional law it is forbidden to pronounce even one word of the Torah publicly unless it is read from the written text. No such instrument is mentioned in ancient literature, and the word took root only in the eighteenth century and even later in the communities of Europe and North Africa. The Yemenites used a similar instrument which they call a *mahaveh*. The *yad* is made of gold, silver, copper, brass, amber, ivory or wood worked in a variety of techniques: filigree, cast, hammered or carved. Some are adorned with pearls, corals and precious stones, others with dedications and appropriate verses. The *yad* evolved from an implement of talmudic times called a stylus, which was used by school children to guide their reading as well as for writing on a wax-covered board.

RIMON (plural RIMONIM; literally pomegranate), an adornment for the *sefer Torah*. In the ancient idolatrous world, the pomegranate was considered a holy tree symbolizing the planet Mars, and its name was used as a suffix to the names of gods such as Hadadrimon (Zechariah 12:11) and Tabrimon (I Kings 15:18). In Greek mythology the pomegranate is associated with Persephone and Hera, symbols of love and fertility, because of its abundant seed. So, too Jewish society of antiquity also used the pomegranate as a gift from the groom to his betrothed.

In Jewish art and in books of the Kabbala, the pomegranate appears in a variety of contexts. It is among the finest fruits of the Land of Israel (Deuteronomy 8:8), is mentioned among decorative articles and is a subject of *midrashic* symbolism and allegory. *Rimonim* of coloured wool, alternating with golden bells, hung at the hem of the High Priest's robe (Exodus 28:33). In the same fashion, something similar to *rimonim* were placed at the top of the priest's headdress. In Solomon's Temple, copper pomegranates adorned the tops of the columns. Three pomegranates are drawn on the ceiling of a third-century synagogue and also appear on Jewish coins from the year 66 CE. The fruit also shows up in mosaic floors and reliefs of ancient synagogues.

In talmudic literature, mention of the pomegranate and the apple (an alternative usage) in the Torah and in connection with the commandments is subject to a variety of interpretations: 'The pomegranates budded forth' (Song of Songs) – these are the children who sit in rows like the seeds of the pomegranate and study the Torah; 'I raised thee up under the apple tree' (*ibid.*) – the apple gives fruit in the month of Sivan, and the Torah was given in the same month; 'Thy temples are like a piece of pomegranate' (*ibid.*) – even the simplest of them are as full of good deeds as a pomegranate is of seeds. In addition, one who sees the pomegranate in a dream is seeing the Torah.

Apparently combining the idea of the High Priest's clothing with such homiletic commentaries, and also associating the pomegranates with the columns of the Temple, Jewish artisans began to create artistic objects in the form of pomegranates to decorate the 'trees of life' of the *sefer Torah*. At first they used a replica of the apple or the pomegranate, but in the course of centuries basic changes took place in line with the taste and fancy of the artists or of the people who commissioned the work. *Rimonim* are made of gold, silver, crystal, brocade, velvet and wood and are shaped like upright crowns, arched towers, round balls, vases and so on.

HITUL, see MAPAH.